WILD TONGUES

WILD TONGUES

A Handbook of
Social Pathology

FRANKLIN H. LITTELL

The Macmillan Company
Collier-Macmillan Ltd., London

FIRST PRINTING

The Macmillan Company
Collier-Macmillan Canada Ltd., Toronto, Ontario

Printed in the United States of America

TO
Thelma Stevens

Contents

●━●

Foreword

THIS *Handbook* IS PREPARED in the conviction that the American experiment in liberty and self-government is facing a time of trial in which faithful Christians have a unique vocation to fulfill. The rise of ideological movements and systems places our constitutional order in question. More than that, the movements of pathological nature challenge the church to be the church, for the record of the twentieth century is plain to read: the totalitarian movements and ideologies are not only a political threat, but a profoundly religious challenge. Where such movements have come to strength or triumph, they have been "post-Christian": that is, they have gained authority as the Christian movement has lost momentum and direction. Put bluntly, both Communist- and fascist-type movements are products of culture-religion in decline.

The challenge of the anti-Christian movements might be met head-on, by presenting a manual of lay training. Well-trained and thoroughly formed Christians do not become Communists, fascists, Mafiosi, or racists.

Correspondence has made clear, however, that—in spite of the extensive records of the church struggle in Communist areas, in the Third Reich of Adolf Hitler, in apartheid South Africa and other sick societies—the growth of attacks on the churches and the Christian gospel has bewildered and confused many Americans. The tactics of the student Maoists and the Church League of America, for example, are not yet recognized for what they are: evidences in America of a malaise which has pervaded Western civilization since World War I.

The church struggle against the adversary poses only to a minor degree the problem of survival in the face of open persecution. Far more fundamental is the problem of dealing with the infiltrator, the apostate, who often uses the church language to tear and rend the Christian movement. This *Handbook* is intended to help sincere Christians who are confused when false prophets use the language of prophecy, the confessions and creeds, Christians orthodoxy, to scandalize the Christian movement by slander and schism.

Because the great Ordinance of Religious Freedom of Virginia and the First Amendment to the federal Constitution separated the religious and political covenants, the student must learn to distinguish the challenge to true religion from the challenge to liberty and self-government. Actually, the threat posed by pathological movements and groups is both religious and political. The answer is not, however, to defend "Christian America" against its enemies. The answers are: to strengthen the Christian movement against apostates and false prophets; to strengthen the liberty and self-government of *all* American citizens against the totalitarian political thrusts.

Both Marxist- and fascist-type movements propose a

return to the old style of uniting religious and political commitments and sanctions. They are regressive rather than "the wave of the future," as they falsely claim. For the true Christian in America, the response must be a double one: to strengthen the discipline and integrity of the Christian covenants and at the same time to welcome the growth of the liberty and dignity of all citizens—regardless of race or creed—in the political covenant. We who love Christ desire no return to the sham of a Christian establishment. We who love liberty desire no return to a religious or ideological monolith. The path of high religion in the years ahead lies along the mountain paths of deeper voluntary effort and devotion. The path of Amerca's political future lies through the highlands of liberty, not the police state.

Although the religious issue is separate from the political, the enemy of both is the same: the pathological totalitarian style, whether radical left or radical right in its posture. Knowing the adversary thoroughly is not only a help to decision but a key to religious and political health. For, as in a good department or school of medicine the study of pathology is of great help in understandng physical health, so the study of social pathology sums up a volume of clues to religious and political well-being.

In closing these opening remarks I would like to express my gratitude to Miss Peggy Billings of the Woman's Division of the United Methodist Church and to Professor Frank Wright, Jr., and Mrs. Jan H. Wright for encouragement and invaluable assistance.

F.H.L.

Iowa Wesleyan College
Mt. Pleasant, Iowa

If, drunk with sight of power, we loose
  Wild tongues that have not thee in awe—
Such boasting as the Gentiles use
  Or lesser breeds without the Law—
Lord God of Hosts, be with us yet,
  Lest we forget—lest we forget!
    from "Recessional," by Rudyard Kipling

WILD TONGUES

I

⚊⚊⚊⚊⚊⚊

Danger in America

⚊⚊⚊⚊⚊⚊⚊⚊⚊⚊⚊⚊⚊⚊⚊⚊⚊⚊

1968

*T*HE year 1968 was without doubt the worst in the
history of America, not excepting the years blemished
by Benedict Arnold's treason, Aaron Burr's conspiracy,
Andersonville, the lynching of Leo Frank, the Palmer
raids and the Teapot Dome Scandal. In that year there
bubbled to the top of the cauldron the most shocking
demonstrations of the American propensity for violence. The murders of Dr. Martin Luther King, Jr.,
and Senator Robert Kennedy were but the appalling
symbols of a political and spiritual sickness which ran
deep in the soul of the people. Its fruits were not only
assassination but ravaged inner cities, pillaged campus
buildings, and the emergence of what for a time
seemed the most serious threat to the American experiment in liberty and self-government since the Civil
War: the George Wallace campaign.

To be sure, the candidacy of a violent racist demagogue whose reputation had been built upon defiance
of the law of the land and of his own state was managed by two prominent fascist-type conspiracies: the
White Citizens' Councils and the John Birch Society.
In twenty-two states the Wallace campaign was managed, the conventions held, and the electors selected
out of the headquarters of the John Birch Society. In
ten states the White Citizens' Councils played a major
role. But George Wallace's appeal ran far deeper and
he managed to collect about himself every one of the
organizations devoted to a rightest coup—from the
paramilitary Minutemen to the night riders of the Ku
Klux Klan. His assault upon the American system and
style of fair play was far more dangerous than that of
other demagogues in this century—such as Senators
Joseph McCarthy of Wisconsin or Tom Watson of
Georgia—not alone because he received better-financed
and disciplined aid from conspirators [1] but because the
modern techniques of mass communication were har-
nessed to old American drives of anti-intellectualism,
anti-foreignism, primitive Protestant bigotry and white
racism.

Across the generations, as might be expected in the
history of a people once controlled by Protestant state
churches and dominated until very recently by a
Protestant social establishment, the most vicious and
reactionary movements have been white, Anglo-Saxon,
and Protestant (WASP). In the last few years there
has emerged an unsavory alliance between Catholic
reaction (e.g. Manion Forum, Cardinal Mindzenty
Foundation, *The Wanderer* newspaper) and some sections of the Protestant radical right. Now some of the

[1] Cf. Appendix 2.

black extremist movements are adopting demagogic politics, secret organizational methods, and violent actions as destructive as those long used by disloyal white groups. But the roots of Amercan disaffection and disloyalty lie deep in the past.

Just as the Nazis found vital contact with the Teutonic folk myth and folk history to be appealing, just as every other national totalitarian movement has found appeal to ethnicity and tribal memory natural and strength-giving, so has it been in America.

The roots of America reach back through the years of Protestant nativism to the days when a family fireside game in New England was "Break the Pope's Neck." Since the abolition of slavery, there has been added to it a strong romantic attachment to the myth of the ante-bellum South—so glamorously portrayed in the movie *Birth of a Nation* and the best seller *Gone with the Wind*.

At its relatively sophisticated level, Protestant nativism rallies to the cause of "Christian America" and heartily condemns religious liberty, cultural pluralism, and social mobility. At its vulgar level, the reactionary myth of the past is backdrop to a demonic racist ideology. Always, covert or overt, the strain of violence is evident.

What is imperative as innoculation against the appeals of a George Wallace or a James Eastland is realization by Christians that modern America is the place of dialogue—a far nobler exercise than the old persecution of dissenters. America is the first authentic World City, where equally "entitled" citizens of the most various backgrounds can learn to live together as truly human. Our faith is far better commended to the others by active love and brotherly service than by resentful recollections of old special privileges! What is imperative is the realization by all men of good will that for the citizenship of any one of us to be secure, all must be protected in their rights and in their persons. For this reason, it is racial justice—the "crisis of conscience" for America—that must at all costs be won. The enemies of liberty and self-government, like all children of darkness so often wiser than the children of light, know that the supreme test lies here. Precisely for this reason, all totalitarian movements in the United States—Communist, fascist, white extremist, and black extremist—attempt to play upon racial prejudice and antagonism.

The Beauty of Pluralism

To accept religious, cultural, and ethnic pluralism as a positive good comes hardest to the Protestants, for they have a group memory of America before the Catholic and Jewish immigrations of the latter half of the nineteenth century changed the face of the American people. And, although most of us would like now to forget it, it was the Protestant "Founding Fathers" who—even at the high point of launching the new nation—failed to deal morally and courageously with slavery, a social cancer which continued to distend until it almost wrecked the United States. Black Americans, overwhelmingly Baptist in religious preference, have never been victimized by the myth of the "good old days." American Catholics and Jews, although some have attempted to develop a life removed from the mainstream, are well aware of the battle of their parents and grandparents to overcome the weight and controls of the once-dominant Protestant establishment. This has made the affirmation of pluralism and its benefits a peculiarly white Protestant problem.

The issue can be refined more than that: the acceptance of the full implications of religious liberty and of the pluralism of religious loyalties and the wide evidence of conscience which naturally go with it are peculiarly a problem for those Protestant churches derived from British Christendom: Anglicans, Congregationalists, Presbyterians, and—especially since their rise to strength in the mass evangelism of the nineteenth century—Baptists, Methodists, and Disciples of Christ. Since the ratification of the First Amendment to the federal Constitution, the legal establishment of any single national church has been prevented. Nevertheless, on the eastern seaboard some states continued to accord a privileged position to one religion or another and, during the nineteenth century, Protestantism enjoyed a pre-eminence in the culture and the public liturgy. It was not until 1912 that the last state constitution removed discriminatory clauses against the Jews. It was not until 1960 that Catholics overcame national political disadvantage, a disadvantage reinforced by prejudice which played a large role in the 1928 election. It was not until the second half of the twentieth century that the courts began to eliminate the last vestiges of the Protestant publc liturgy from the public schools.

Until 1820, 85 percent of the American people were descended from British stock, and for more than a century longer a social establishment (no longer strictly legal) continued the mind-set of British Christendom. The great revival churches of the nineteenth century— Baptists, Methodists, and Disciples of Christ—perpetuated the social establishment of religion which gave credibility to the myth of "Christian America." Nevertheless, their evangelists operated on the assumption shown correct by actual statistics of church membership: that North America was a mission field like Africa or Asia.

The minor religious groups of the colonial period championed religious liberty, voluntary membership, and pluralism even while the Anglican and Congregational state churches sought to enforce legal uniformity. Quakers and Brethren and Mennonites, in Europe as well as America, opposed the whole myth of "Christendom." German-language groups like the Lutherans and Reformed have never anticipated the opportunity to dominate or control religious life in America, and they were long blocked from the mainstream by foreign-language worship and culture. But the large Protestant churches of British background—even the Baptists and Methodists and Disciples of Christ when they grew large and prosperous as a result of the revivals of religion—have, like the Presbyterians, repeatedly been drawn into support of the myth of "Christian America" and established religion.

The confusion prevailing among many Protestants came to the fore in recent attacks on the Supreme Court for "taking God out of the schoolroom." Almost all of the so-called "Prayer Amendments," supported by some men of stature as well as by all of the representatives of the spiritual underworld, carried revealing demurrers to the effect that no discrimination toward —much less persecution of—religious minorities was intended. In a society truly devoted to religious liberty— a different thing from toleration—such demurrers are superfluous, indeed presumptuous.

What the Supreme Court decisions have done, be-

latedly, is to draw the logical and necessary consequences of the First Amendment. The enforcement of
the Constitution has given a chance for disloyal and
bigoted politicians to attack the Supreme Court as
"atheistic," "un-Godly," or "irreligious." Some ultra-
conservatives like Senator Dirksen of Illinois have
joined forces with radical rightists like Governors Wallace and Maddox to overthrow the Court's authority
and/or to defy the law of the land outright.

The twin forces that most confuse the present scene
and polarize the unwary between a militant secularism
which would deny the free exercise of religion and a
conservative defense of the old Protestant tradition,
which amounts to an establishment of religion, however
"nonsectarian," are still alive and divisive to America.
The Hamden Christmas observance case of 1961 is as
good an illustration as any of how the liberty accorded
to both church and state in our system may *not* be
served.

As the Christmas season of 1961 approached, the traditional preparations were made for hymn sings and
Christmas pageantry in the schools of Hamden, Con-
necticut. But this time their continuance was chal-
lenged:. the New Haven Jewish Community Council
released a public statement calling on fellow citizens
"to guard with scrupulous care the high wall of separation between church and state erected by the Founding
Fathers." Thus aroused by challenge to unthinking
custom, the priest at St. Rita's Church and a local
Protestant pastor rose to defend "Christian America"
from their pulpits. On December 4 a Protestant ser-
mon, with suitable press releases, declared that "cul-
turally the United States of America is Christian" and
that "when any people become so divisive that they re-

fuse to listen to the prayers and songs and traditions of another's faith, then God is becoming a distant reality." [2]

Both postures were ideological rather than historical and neighborly, and months of hard work were required to knit the community back together after the mutual recriminations. The Christian spokesmen were quite right that there had been Christmas observances in the public schools of New Haven since long before there was a United States of America and that a "high wall of separation" was something neither they nor their fathers had even intended. The Jewish Community Council was quite right in feeling that religious exercises in public institutions which may have been valid in early times were no longer appropriate or just in a pluralistic society.

The truth is that the "Founding Fathers" neither intended nor erected a high wall of separation between church and state. Nor did they establish a Christian nation, for basic religious commitment is not subject to legislation. We are moving forward, in American history, to strengthen *voluntary* religion. The proper role of government is to stay out of the business of religion and to get out of it where the momentum of an earlier tradition of culture-religion still hangs on as a culture lag. There is no concern of high level religion which cannot stand the open competition with alternative orders of being. Even the former ethnic religions, Buddhism and Hinduism and Islam, are now sending out missionaries to Europe and North America.[3] Signifi-

[2] Cf. *Background Reports*, edited by Arthur Gilbert (New York: National Conference of Christians and Jews, June, 1962).
[3] Kurt Hutten and Siegfried von Kortzfleisch, eds., *Asien Missioniert im Abendland* (Stuttgart: Kreuz-Verlag, 1963), *passim*.

cantly, it is the renewal movements in those faith groupings which are now entering into competition for the voluntary decisions of the common men of many nations.

The government which best serves the Ages of Dialogue is not, then, one which strives in some fashion to maintain a diluted public liturgy—clinging lingeringly to what is left of a deracinated Christendom. Such retrogressive political actions serve neither God nor man. The best government is that which, shunning ideology, maintains the order and peace within which fellow-citizens may—in the field of religion as in other matters affecting their destiny—engage in full, free, and informed public discussion, and then act in consensus.

The cultural anti-Semitism which infects "Christian America" was dramatically demonstrated again during a school board election at Wayne, New Jersey, in 1967. A bond issue was at stake. Five candidates, two of them Jews, were running for three vacancies. Newton Miller, vice-president of the board and bitterly opposed to the bond issue, released an anti-Semitic attack on the Jewish candidates one week before the election. As carried with banner headlines the next day, he warned:

> Most Jewish people are liberals, especially when it comes to spending for education. If Kraus and Mandell are elected . . . and Fred Lafer [a Jewish board member not up for re-election] is in for two more years, that's a three-to-six vote. It would only take two more votes for a majority, and Wayne would be in real financial trouble . . .
>
> Two more votes and we lose what is left of Christ in our Christmas celebrations in our schools. Think of it.[4]

[4] R. Stark and S. Steinberg, *It Did Happen Here* (Berkeley: Univ. of Calif. Press, 1967), p. 3.

The voters did and went 3 to 1 against the candidates who were identified as Jews, and the school budget lost.

The incident is representative on several scores. In the first place, no church leaders and no denominations (with the possible exception of a few defrocked preachers and marginal sects rallying to culture-religion in what is presumptuously called "the American Council of Churches") would make such a "Christian" statement as Miller's, and none approved it once made. Neither do responsible church groups advocate retention of the old Protestant religious exercises in today's public schools: quite the contrary. But Miller represented that backwash of vaguely Christian culture-religion which is the fertile source of racism, anti-Semitism, and fascist-type politics in America. Disloyal to the church's own stand, and playing upon the most wicked prejudice of twentieth-century politics, Miller was able to effect a reactionary political triumph by using "Christian" appeal to produce an anti-Christian response. His success shows up again the dangers of culture-religion on which Hitler and the German Christians also built (temporarily) successful low-grade politics. The successful misuse of "Christian" appeals shows two basic faults in the church: (1) the church's lack of "offense" to the spirit of the times; (2) the church's lack of internal integrity, reinforced by church discipline.

Since the church herself maintains promiscuous membership, and refuses to draw a frontier line between her own views and those of the age, she cannot plead innocent when anti-Semitism and other anti-Christian motifs flourish among her weaker constituents.

The age of pluralism marks the end of monologue

and the featuring of dialogue. But even dialogue has its limits: some truths can only be acted, not uttered. In a very real sense, this is the Age of the Laity—the age when the faith affirmation becomes credible by reason of faithful action rather than verbal expression. A brilliant theologian of the *diakonia* had put the matter this way:

> In the service of love of the brother, the sacramental element is foremost; it is the life of the Christian Community and its integrity which is at stake.
>
> In the service of love of the neighbor, the proclamation is expressed in non-verbal ways; action speaks louder than words, but it is Christ who is proclaimed.
>
> In the service of love of the stranger (*Fernenliebe*), the proclamation plays no role as yet; through prayer and trust in the often hidden work of the Holy Spirit, Christian service is linked to God's will for the whole world.[5]

To these expanding circles of perception may be added another important dimension: the wisdom to perceive and welcome truth even when it is performed under nonreligious auspices altogether.

The pluralistic setting is one in which a heavy premium is placed on the credible deed, the action backed by integrity of church life and commitment. A formal and verbal orthodoxy, to which the society is ostensibly bound, has with the end of the Constantinian era become both incredible and unworthy. Churchmen must again take seriously the possibility that they, and their boards and agencies and tables of conformity, must,

[5] P. J. R. Abbing, "Grundlinien zu einer theologischen Lehre vom Diakanat," *L Monatsschrift für Pastoraltheologie* (1961) 9:354f.

like their Master, go to the Cross for the sake of the salvation of the world.

As racial strife has come to the fore, and also as a result of the 1960 presidential election, the religious conflict has somewhat receded. But the danger of pathological corruption is still present.

The Preliminary Stages of a Church Struggle

In point of fact the churches, which played a notable role in arousing the conscience of America on the significance of practical brotherhood between citizens of all cultures, races, and religions, are under savage attack from the fascist side.

In October of 1966, the author was privileged to lecture at the annual Ministers' Conference at Andover Newton Theological School on the growth of extremist groups and organizations in America. The lecture was subsequently published in *Andover Newton Quarterly*,[6] and one of the numerous letters of comment is so representative as to bear quotation at length:

> I have just receved a copy of the *Andover Newton Quarterly*, and have read with a very personal concern the lecture on "The Growing Church Struggle in America" which you presented at my *alma mater* on last October 19. The poignancy of the problem which you have addressed, and the careful articulation of both its symptoms and its possible effects, compel me, even at the risk of seeming presumptuous, to write you. (I deeply regret that I was unable to attend the lecture.)

[6] Vol. VII, No. 3, pp. 113–26.

The thesis of your lecture has been thoroughly confirmed in my personal experience since coming to the pastorate of this church in 1963. I am certain, however, that some of my colleagues minimize the intractability of extremist thought and the seriousness of its threat to our liberties. For whatever value it may have, I offer the following:

On Sunday morning, October 25, 1964, three men interrupted our worship during the time of the pastoral prayer, prevented the organist from playing the hymn at the close of the prayer, and proceeded to read from the choir position a statement charging that materials produced by the National Council of Churches and the United Church of Christ are "immoral," "atheistic," and "Communistic." The statement suggested the identification of all who used any materials published by either group as Communists themselves, and demanded the immediate dismissal of the minister on those grounds. (It happened that none of the publications which the extremist faction later identified as "immoral" or "communistic" had actually been used in this church!) The struggle of faith which followed assumed community-, and even area- and state-, proportions as party leaders in this congregation lit similar fires in other churches as far as ninety miles away. The trauma lasted here for approximately one year, during which our sermons were secretly taped for criticism by the John Birch Society, unanticipated calls at the parsonage issued in various threats, and the charge of being communistic was used to the point of absurdity.

Your lecture so well clarifies what my experience has borne out—namely, that extremism is symptomatic of a defect in personality or spirit, and that the power of reason is virtually ineffective in any direct confrontation. When we have attempted to use reason with such persons, our words and intentions have been invariably perverted; any effort to express Christian charity has been taken as evidence of weakness.

Help came to our situation when revulsion from the sick spirit of the extremists became serious enough to incite the other members of the church to act upon their faith. This church would certainly have passed into the control of members of the John Birch Society had not the situation been taken seriously at the time of crisis.

It has been approximately one year since the crisis situation in this church ended. (It ended with the withdrawal of some thirty members who, with other disaffected persons from the local Methodist, Nazarene and Baptist churches, founded a fundamentalist church of the most extreme character. Inspiration for the organization of the church came in part through a present associate of Carl McIntire.) In that time we have come to observe the development of a new kind of danger in this congregation—the tendency, now that the extremists are no longer working from within the fellowship, to minimize the hazard which the continued propagation of extremist thought in the community poses for the future.

Many ministers of my acquaintance have already dealt squarely with the problems which extremism has created. I am alarmed, however, by the number of both ministers and laymen whose idealism seems to prevent a realistic encounter with this illness of our society.

It has been most gratifying to learn of the organization of the Institute for American Democracy, Inc.[7] I should be pleased to be counted as a friend to your purposes, and to have my name placed on your mailing list.

By dealing with the problem of extremism at that level at which it most vitally affects our work and our future, you have put those of us who labor in the pastorate very much in your debt.

Such a letter hardly needs comment, since it portrays

[7]Cf. Appendix 3 for information on IAD.

so vividly the wretchedness caused in hundreds of churches by followers of the false prophets. ("False Christs and false prophets will arise and show signs and wonders, to lead astray, if possible, the elect." Mark 13:22)

Nevertheless, to make the point plain, those who attempted to split the congregation were guilty of a series of sins more grievous than lack of civilized manners. Among the more evident are these: irreverence, slander, lying, deceit, violence, conspiracy, schism. In the Early Church, persons who so conducted themselves were charged with breaking the covenant of faith and refusing to "hear the Church" (called "the sin against the Holy Spirit," Acts 5:1–11), and, if they remained obdurate, they were expelled. John Wesley and his men were also strict disciplinarians, for they took seriously the truth of the general priesthood of believers: that in the end we must answer for each other's blood. A major occasion of our present difficulties, in the large and successful Protestant denominations, is precisely the abandonment of any membership standards or procedures of Christian discipline.

This point was brought vividly home to me in another exchange of letters, an exchange with a very perceptive lay woman in Cedar Rapids, Iowa, which followed on my address at the National Conference on Religion and Race (Chicago: January 15, 1963). The exchange follows:

Cedar Rapids, Iowa
February 23, 1963

Dear Sir:

Recently I read in the Cedar Rapids Gazette that you have posed the question: "Should churches purge their membership rolls of those whose lives flagrantly contradict the teachings of Christ?" I inferred from the remarks credited to you that you believe that this sort of discipline would aid the church in working for social justice.

In the first place, I think that the struggle for social justice ought to be carried on by Christians—as individuals—and not by the church as such.

In the second place, it seems to me that the church is too involved in social and business activities to attend properly to its primary purpose of making Christians of us. What greater evidence is there of this than the existence of the hypocrites you would expel? The lines of communication between God and man seem to be in need of repair.

I have talked with several ministers about membership standards. Not one agrees with you. If a man's actions are to be regulated by imposed discipline, rather than self-discipline, the church may become an exclusive club of those who sin the least conspicuously.

Cordially,
M—— W——

February 27, 1963
Dear Mrs. W——:

Thank you for your letter of February 23rd. My reference to the need for a recovery of church discipline dealt not only with the social action issue, but also with the general need for stronger missionary support, a higher level of marriage and family morals, and the rest of the factors involved in a Christian style of living. The greatest scandal in America today is the lack of a practice of biblical "separation" of the church from the world, and this shows at every level. I'm sorry that the preachers you spoke to failed to recognize the importance of a Christian style of life: this is all the more evidence of the point I am making, which is that we have bought statistical success at the price of sacrificing membership stands. There is no doubt whatever as to what Martin Luther, John Calvin, John Knox, John Wesley or any of the other great Christian statesmen would have thought of this. The church is of course not supposed to be "an exclusive club," since it is open to those who are repentant and intend to lead a new life. But it certainly is not supposed to be a promiscuous civic assembly either! I think the Bible is quite clear on this point.

Sincerely yours,
Franklin H. Littell
Professor

Cedar Rapids, Iowa
March 1, 1963

Dear Professor Littell:

Thank you for your reply to my letter.

I do not feel that the fact that certain ministers disagreed with you about the establishment of membership standards suggests that they have "failed to recognize the importance of a Christian style of life." The history of Christianity abounds with controversy over methods of achieving agreed-upon goals. Martin Luther, John Calvin and John Wesley may all have agreed upon this point, but the existence of the separate churches which they represented is evidence that there were points upon which they did not agree.

Some of the questions raised were: Are errors of omission to be treated as harshly as those of commission? What constitutes "flagrant contradiction"? Will good acts be balanced against bad ones? Is there a time limit on repentance? One minister said that no one is taken off the membership rolls of his church for any reason other than transfer or death. In his words, "I am willing to wait all a man's life for him to repent. That maturity which results in responsible action comes early to some, late to others, depending upon the conditions which are peculiar to his life." Another minister suggested that a purge of membership rolls would be a violation of the words of Jesus, to wit: "Judge not, that ye be not judged"; "Let him who is without sin cast the first stone"; "Ye (shall forgive them) seventy times seven times." To rebuke is one thing, to expel another.

If members were to join the church because of a commitment, it might be proper to hold them accountable to the church for their actions. But many —perhaps most—join because of a desire to conform to an accepted custom. As Vance Packard says, "Most people vote for the same reason they go to church— it's the thing to do." And since the prevailing opinion among respectable people seems to be "it doesn't matter where you go to church—just so you go," the choice of church is often governed by family custom, locale, "friendliness" of the congregation, personality of the minister, etc., rather than an examination of the principles to which the particular sect adheres. It seems to me then that the purpose of the church is not only to seek conversion of members *to* the church, but also to seek conversion of members *in* the church.

Is the church meeting the latter challenge? I don't think so. The principles of the Christian religion are assumed to be understood and accepted by members, which is not necessarily so, and they are directed to the overt work of the church. The expulsion of some members for flagrant sins will not aid the cause of converting so-called Christians to Christianity, but will only instill in them a desire to conform to a "Christian style of life" for the wrong reason—to maintain respectability.

I do not understand what you mean by "a practice of biblical 'separation' of the church from the world." But since I do not want to impose upon your time, perhaps you might have one of your students answer this for me, if there is someone so inclined.

Cordially,

M—— W——

March 12, 1963

Dear Mrs. W——:

Thank you for your very intelligent and perceptive letter of March 1st. I think you have stated the situation exactly the way it is, and in doing so have described an established church. The arguments which were put forward against church discipline are precisely the arguments which are given by our brethren of the church of Sweden, the church of Hanover, the church of Wurttemberg and of the Catholic church in France and Italy against effort to establish standards of membership. They feel that they owe the whole population something which is called "Christian service," and consequently they're not willing to emphasize the covenant or separation or any of the other classical Free Church principles. If your library has a copy of my book published in 1957 called *The Free Church* (Beacon Press), you'll find considerable detail as to the way in which religious liberty and voluntaryism are tied up with the matter of church discipline. There is, of course, a great deal to be said in favor of Christendom and religious establishment; but we should be aware that it's an entirely different Christianity from our heritage as children of fathers who believed in integrity of membership, religious voluntaryism and religious liberty.

Sincerely yours,
Franklin H. Littell
Professor

Perhaps the most revealing sentence of all was the phrase in the fourth paragraph of her second letter: "If members were to join the church because of a commitment . . ." This is the crux of the matter. Officially, at least, members still join with promise to maintain a style of life and conduct worthy of the name. But since the bars have been let down, and most join the socially established churches for reasons of social identity; those who argue for promiscuity of membership find popular support. But how much slander and lying, how frequent arson of Negro churches, how much murder or beating of the helpless, how active a disloyalty to the church and its leadership must be borne before the question is raised whether such person is no longer in good standing in the Covenant? (Matt. 18:15–19)

The Ninth Commandment has not been repealed: "You shall not bear false witness against your neighbor." (Exod. 20:16)

The New Testament rule still stands, intended precisely to block the influence of false prophets:

"Never admit any charge against an elder except on the evidence of two or three witnesses." (I Tim. 5:19, II Cor. 13:1)

And for the activities of the extremists in the churches there is a tailormade proverb:

> There are six things which the Lord hates,
>   seven which are an abomination to him:
> haughty eyes, a lying tongue,
>   and hands that shed innocent blood,
> a heart that devises wicked plans,
>   feet that make haste to run to evil,
> a false witness who breathes out lies,
>   and a man who sows discord among brethren.
>   (Prov. 6:16–19)

If we turn again to the extremist demagogues and their effort to create disloyalty and schism in the churches, what do we find but false prophets?—a Carl McIntire, defrocked for conduct unworthy of a minister, who has devoted his life to splitting churches in Korea, South Africa, Germany, the United States; a Stewart McBirnie; a Billy James Hargis, who calls himself "Reverend" and "Doctor," although no denomination claims him and no reputable institution known to me has given him a degree; an Edgar Bundy, who runs a front for the John Birch Society called "Church League of America," with the assignment to attack church leaders and the ecumenical movement! The Ku Klux Klan, a murderous conspiracy, opens its meetings with prayer; has "blasphemy" no meaning any more?

In many congregations in America we are today facing precisely the same kind of two-pronged attack and infiltration which made so many German Christians apostatize and become fellow travelers to Nazism, which has softened up many Polish Catholics and East German Protestants to accommodation to Marxism. It is the sickness of Christendom that so many of the baptized, poorly trained, and ill-disciplined, under pressure and temptation, go over to the adversary.

The Imperative:
A Recovery of Christian Discipline

The light-hearted attitude toward lack of standards of church membership, one of the chief marks of legally and/or socially established religion, has never characterized Christians in earnest. The totalitarian movements have arisen in the heart of Christendom among ill-trained baptized, the observers of culture-religion who, under pressure or temptation, go over to the adversary. The extremist threat in America is strongest precisely in those great areas of culture-religion where church discipline has fallen into disuse.

Communism and fascism involve both faithless beliefs and faithless action, and those who attempt to retain church membership and Christian appearance while serving other masters are heretics. As Professor Graham Taylor of Chicago put it long ago, the deliberate "choice of actions which are not only in known opposition to the law of God and the practice of the church" is heresey. And he went on to write, "Worse is it to live heresy than to believe it, not only because the intrinsic wrong is greater, but because the resulting evils are more widespread and disastrous." [8]

Those who oppose membership training and membership standards for the sake of a shallow satistical show of success, and they have been many in recent years, are actually preparing the weak "soldiers of Christ" for defection and the strong for suffering and defeat.

Contrary to some claims, the Marxist lands do not allow religious liberty. Neither do they tolerate churches which maintain discipline and standards of membership.

The assertion that religious liberty exists in the USSR—or even a meaningful toleration—is a patent fraud, however often repeated by Communists, fellow travelers, or well-meaning persons attempting to make coexistence more attractive. Article 124 of the Constitution of 1918 affirmed the right to "freedom of worship and of anti-religious propaganda"—but not of religious propaganda. In a 1924 law, religious associations are forbidden to:

> A. Establish welfare funds, cooperatives, production associations and, generally, use the funds at their disposal for any purpose other than meeting the exigencies connected with religion and worship.
> B. Lend material aid to their members, to organize

[8] Cf. *Christian Intelligence* (May 23, 1879), Vol. XLIX, p. 1.

prayer groups of children, young people or women, and, generally, to organize meetings, clubs, cells or centers for biblical, literary, trade, professional, religious, etc. studies. . . .

In the penal code there are stiff penalties provided for "religious instruction given to children or young people in educational institutions and public or state schools . . . collections taken for the support of ecclesiastical or religious groups. . . ."

Although the dictator, Stalin, found it expedient to appeal to religious sentiment in the war against Nazism, and although in recent years some Russian Orthodox delegates have been allowed to attend international church gatherings, the basic state policy remains unchanged: the established cult, Marxism, is enforced and reinforced by law in a permanent policy of throttling active religion and stifling live faith.

It should not be forgotten that dissenting Christians and Jews were also savagely persecuted and put to death under the Tsars, and with the blessing of the leaders of the privileged Orthodox establishment. The Communist rulers have simply continued the old policies of repression and included the Orthodox, too.

Fascists argue from Communist repression of religion that "Christian" governments should favor Christianity and use political power to advance Christian ideology over Marxism. They also argue that "atheistic" governments should be excluded from the United Nations and that they cannot be trusted in other treaty agreements. This is a specious and unrealistic argument, confusing Christian and political issues. It would be difficult if not impossible to prove that national governments which pretend to a Christian ideologically are any less self-serving than those frankly atheistic. A

United Nations which can embrace Voerster's South Africa or Nasser's Egypt is certainly broad enough to admit Mao's China. DeGaulle's France and Communist Russia have this in common with other national governments: they will keep agreements so long as it serves their interest, and they break them—if they can get away with it—when they become disadvantageous. The art of politics is precisely to make the continuance of agreements mutually advantageous and their breach painful. The religious encounter is not to be resolved at the level of ideology, and certainly not by government action. The Word of God, which quickens faith, needs only the sword of the spirit.

The believing Christian will pray for his persecuted brethren in Communist or fascist or Muslim territory, where governmental coercion is wrongly used to suppress conscience and faithful witness; he will cultivate both old and new ways of strengthening those in suffering; he will pray that dictators be brought low and liberty flourish; he will not, however, if his mind and spirit are shaped by the God of the Bible, make a superficial identification of national or ethnic interests with Christianity. He will not preach a holy war of "Christian America" against "atheistic Russia" and "Red China," for he knows that America is not yet Christian, and he knows that God's common grace is working even in Russia and China. He knows that in spiritual warfare the approved weapon is "the Sword of the Spirit which is the Word of God" (Eph. 6:17), not the atom bomb.

Racial Tension

The major tension area in America shifted from interreligious conflict to racial tension during the last decade of action and court decision to end second-class citizenship.

The fight of American Negroes to achieve full citizenship after a century of official emancipation also has sharpened the issue between those who look backward to the "good old days" and those who appreciate the beauties of pluralism and the grandeur of open-faced dialogue. In the same week that he attacked the Supreme Court for enforcing the First Amendment, Senator Dirksen joined the white supremacists in sabotaging the ill-fated Civil Rights Act of 1965. A southern politician let the cat out of the bag when he attacked the Supreme Court for shutting God out of the schoolroom and letting the "nigras" in. The battle for the liberty and dignity of all citizens has thus become increasingly tainted by the racist ideology of the radical right, an ideology which—backstopped by a myth of the "good old days"—attracts the support of the misguided religious as well as the wickedly bigoted. Since 1954 there has been founded a network of independent churches and "Churches of Christian Liberty," dedicated to white and "Christian" power. Private and "Christian" schools have been founded, and in some cases supported by tax monies, to defy the law of the land.

The disappointment of black citizens has been profound as they see quiet defiance of the law still being carried on by politicians sworn to uphold the Constitution and as many of their leaders have been mur-

dered with impunity and their murderers unpursued or
let go free. Furthermore, the flight of southern Negroes
into the central city of northern metropolises has
locked them into physical conditions far more cruel
than most of the rural Southland. Coming north in
hope, they have found the politicians and police just
as corrupt and brutal and the school and employment
situations in the main just as dark as the "Egypt" from
which they took their exodus.

With the murder of Dr. King, apostle of nonviolence, the time ran out on peaceful change, and black
extremism began to claim Negro youth and students.
Among able youth, few are going to seminary, though
the church was once the center of black community
life. The debate is right now raging between integration and apartheid, with the hostiles preferring Afro-
Americanism and black militancy to the moderation
and balanced views of veterans of the struggle for racial
justice like Roy Wilkins, James Farmer, and Whitney
Young. If the black militants with the ideological
weaponry and toughness of Muhammed Ali and
Robert Williams and LeRoi Jones win out, "Whitey"
may yet come to realize that, in the death of Martin
Luther King, Jr., he lost his best friend. For the real
militants, and they are found in every city and on almost every campus in America, are just as determined
to burn and to tear and to destroy—before building on
new lines, yet unclear—as are the Communists and
fascists.

Racial militancy is allied with leftist cadres in the
major centers of campus unrest, although their sepa-
ratist ideology ironically puts them much closer to the
apartheid philosophy of the radical right. In any case,
it is clear that the racism of rebellious black citizens—

often accompanied by anti-Semitism—is a significant force. It is not as dangerous or as poisonous yet as a century of Ku Klux Klan and White Citizens' Council white racism, nor has it anything like the murders, arson, cross burnings, beatings, and subversion of republican politics to its score card; but the tumor is growing, and whether it can be excised by the speedy initiation of wise and just political and economic policies remains doubtful at best.

Totalitarianism on Campus

The newspapers and magazines are full of reports from all over the world indicating that students in Madrid, Prague, Berkeley, Tokyo, and elsewhere are demonstrating against their governors and their lot. In every country, whether Communist or Catholic or "secular," there are those to whom the solution is to call out the police or the army and to suppress the protests. In some areas there is still an effort made to understand what is happening on campus and what the students are trying to say.

The effort to make sense of student protest is increasingly difficult because of the polarization process that is going on. Administrative rigidity, often reinforced by structures of authority which have changed little or none for centuries, is met by ideological cadres slanted more and more toward revolution. In the last two years, for instance, the earlier openness and spontaneity of the "new left" has been heavily loaded down with sectarian political ideology and conspiratorial discipline. But dialogue is impossible where encounters are reduced to raw power, where ideology has produced minds closed to the creative spirit, where the balance wheel of dialogue with the past has been lost from the machine.

Academies are especially vulnerable to arbitrary misuse of power by administrations or terrorization by radical cadres because they exaggerate the importance of the spoken or written word and deprecate the importance of structures, power, and violence. The tendency is in part professionally induced and in part due to the fact that civilized men become unfit for survival in a jungle contest of brute force.

For various reasons, not all of which can be treated here, the campuses are becoming the major centers of social conflict in American society. The pressure point has shifted from religious conflict to racist conflict and now to confrontation on campus. There is good reason to suppose that, as things are now shaping up, the campuses will in the coming decade be far more explosive than the black ghettos and slums of the inner city.

In terms of our study of social pathology, the polarization process has advanced in many places to the point where moderation and reason are crushed between fascist elements who advocate smashing student and/or faculty dissent by using off-campus police and Communist and black militant cadres among students and teaching assistants who are attempting revolution on campus.

San Francisco State College is an illustration and a symbol of the developing tragedy. Six or seven years ago, an intelligent administration might have seen the crisis coming and provided the structures and procedures to prevent disaster. Today a tough little scholar of international reputation, Dr. S. I. Hayakawa, is attempting to keep the school going with a minimum of police action: the day is long gone when the necessity of police force could have been avoided. Confronting him is a formation of ideologically tainted and disciplined young revolutionaries, numbering between sixty and three hundred in the inner core (among several thousand registered students), who intend to destroy the institution if they can. The key cadres are Black Student Union and the Third World Liberation Front —Maoist, pro-Viet Cong, and, above all, anti-liberal.

Like the radical right, the Communists and black racists hate "liberals" and moderates worse than anyone else. Although the fascists, in their attempt to polarize and gain followers, verbally attack "liberals," "socialists," and "Communists," and although the pathological movements of the left in their attempt to polarize and gain followers verbally attack "liberals," "bourgeois," and "fascists," both concentrate in fact on breaking the back of moderation—whether "liberal" or "conservative." Both resent, above all, the thought of orderly change, change which can take place without their seizure of power.

The experience of Professor John H. Bunzel of the San Francisco State College faculty is a case in point. Professor Bunzel has had a reputation for years as a "liberal": that is, he has over the years opposed the rightists and stood up for the constitutional rights of Negro citizens. He might well be called a "conservative" for the same reasons, since a person who stands for equal justice before the law and for enforcement of the Constitution is only a "liberal" to fascists. Today he is a "fascist scab" to the leftist student cadres at San Francisco State, simply because he has defended orderly change and the integrity of the academic community. His life has been threatened, the tires of his car slashed, and a bomb planted outside the office of the political science department, which he heads. His home has had to have police protection for months. Students under revolutionary discipline have packed his classes, shouted him down, and prevented his lecturing and conduct of courses. The reason lies not with his personality or competence; it lies with the pathological "worsism" of leftist revolutionaries. Professor Bunzel is defending the right to say or write what he pleases and to teach his classes, "the irreducible minimum of academic freedom." His attackers are ideologically driven. As one said, "He's a much more dangerous thing than a man like George Wallace. With Wallace, everyone knows where he stands. But when Bunzel says something, people say, yeah, he's a liberal so that must be right." [9] People may say it is "liberal" but Professor Bunzel is engaged in an effort which is actually conservative: he is trying to conserve academic freedom, the integrity of the campus, and the possibility for rational and orderly change.

Professor Bruno Bettelheim of the University of Chicago has recently analyzed the alienated students of the radical left and compared their paranoia to that of the German students who helped destroy the Weimar Republic. He thinks it difficult to say whether the disturbances will decline or "lead to a fascism of the Left, like V.I. Lenin and Stalin, or a fascism of the Right, like Hitler. Because in the early days, before the Nazis took over the universities, the Communists tried to take them over. For a time it was hit or miss who would win—the fascists of the Left or the fascists of the

[9] "Harassment Sans Liberal," a special report by Rasa Gustaitis in the Washington *Post*, 2/27/69, p. G3.

Right." [10] Dr. Bettelheim goes on in his discussion to attribute student alienation among the revolutionary cadres to lack of strong paternal authority and clear structures in the homes. Whatever the cause or causes, and in spite of his ambivalent use of the term "fascist," Dr. Bettelheim has put his finger on the precise point at issue: the integrity of the campus is threatened by pathological attacks—of the same kind and style—from both left and right.

During the recent controversy at Harvard, which involved sit-ins on the faculty and protests against a course, "An End to Urban Violence," President Pusey issued a statement which summed up the crisis. He referred to "the ancient privilege of the teacher to teach and the student to learn in an atmosphere of free inquiry and discussion," and went on to comment: "In earlier periods the chief threats to a university's liberty and integrity seem always to have come from outside. The irony and tragedy of the present is that most of the treats to academic liberty and integrity often come from within . . . growing numbers of students have chosen to exercise their frustrations in the academic arena in insufficient awareness of what a university properly is, and sometimes at the expense of the rights of others. Harvard has the right to expect that the members of its faculties and the great majority of its students will have sufficient understanding, historical sense, reason, and self-control to insist that coercive methods have no place in this university community." [11]

In another place something must be said about the way in which violence-prone student cadres learned

[10] Psychiatrist Looks at Protesters," a report by William Braden in the Des Moines *Register*, 3/2/69, p. 1f.

[11] The *Harvard Crimson*, 2/19/69, p. 1.

their tactics in demonstrations and voter-registration campaigns in the Deep South, 1964–67. There, in risk of life and liberty, hundreds of idealistic young Americans faced the police-state practices of racist state and local governments. In that effort, hundreds were jailed illegally, dozens were beaten, and several were murdered. To this must be added the disillusionment of thousands in the major political party conventions of 1968 and the tragedy of the Vietnam War which the youths were the first to see and to feel and to mobilize against. Attacking now the more open sections of the society, the new left students have an easier adversary, one ill-equipped and greatly disinclined to meet their violence with violence. Those who adopt Maoist ideology, discipline, and tactics have become part of the problem. Somehow the substantial majority of students must be won from indifference to a sturdy defense of the liberty and integrity of the campus, or the colleges and universities in America will fall victim to outside attack and inner betrayal.

Among the organized centers of student alienation and revolutionary tactics, the SDS has become best known to the public. The Students for a Democratic Society emerged in the fall of 1961 as a new center of student militancy. Its early bodies broke away from the youth section of the League for Industrial Democracy, and old line Socialist (non-Communist) organization dating back nearly half a century. Inspired by the student freedom marchers and voter-registration drives led by the Student Nonviolent Coordinating Committee (SNCC), they proposed to broaden student action beyond the issue of racial justice to a more general critique of the American culture and economy. A platform was adopted at a national conference of undergraduates meeting in Port Huron, Michigan, in June of 1962. The Port Huron *Statement* stated these basic goals:

> We seek the establishment of a democracy of individual participation with two central aims: that the individual share in those social decisions determining the quality and direction of his life, and that society be organized to encourage independence in men and to provide the media for their common participation.

These directives are no more radical than the Declaration of Independence, and in fact the initial SDS thrust was a good deal less revolutionary than Thomas Jefferson's 1776 manifesto.

The new left has been the despair of disciplined revolutionaries like the Communists, as well as an irritation to the "Establishment." Emphasizing the individual, accenting spontaneity of thought and action, loosely organized in membership, defending the autonomy of local chapters, SDS has been more like traditional American populism than Communist or fascist totalitarianism. It has rapidly grown to about three hundred campus chapters with some 30,000 members and has chiefly gained prominence when some vigorous personality like Tom Hayden has used its sounding board for strong statements against the Establishment, or when some local chapter has forced a confrontation with administrators on a single campus. Since 1963 it has been increasingly involved in organizing slum communities, in opposing the Vietnam War, and in founding "Free Universities" on about one hundred campuses.

From the beginning, SDS opened its membership to all, and in some situations Communists under discipline have been able to use the wider forum effectively.

Moreover, there are increasing evidences of a shift "from dissent to resistance" with—among other actions —sit-ins on draft boards, in college administration buildings, etc. Ideological blocs of all kinds are building up in the formerly inchoate new left, not all by any means clearly Communist, but all making an open dialogue increasingly difficult. A present leader, Carl Davidson, is author of *The Multiversity: Crucible of the New Working Class*—a much more clearly ideological and pro-revolutionary document than the earlier statements of the movement.

A unique strength of SDS has been the willingness of capable organization and field workers—at one point numbering as many as three hundred—to live very simply and work with little or no compensation (an average of less than twenty dollars per week). It should not be forgotten that many of the initial leaders were students jailed illegally—and some beaten or murdered —for their part in the campaigns to register Negro voters in the deep South. This selflessness appeals to youth and students, and it helped to inspire the thousands of young volunteers who mounted the McCarthy campaign in the race for delegates before the 1968 Chicago Democratic Convention.

The machine's victory over Senator McCarthy certainly helped to radicalize the movement, and to turn its spokesmen more bitterly against the Establishment —an omnibus term including college presidents, corporation executives, and leaders of the national government. In recent months the SDS has been evident in harsh confrontations at Columbia University, San Francisco State College, and elsewhere. It is evident that, allied with young black militants who have written the system off, the new left now represents a revolutionary potential not present in its formation or original charter. Some campus groups have recently (in the fall of 1968) become disaffiliated because of the actions of what they call "Maoist-Marxist" cadres seeking control of the movement.

In terms of the totalitarianism "grid," [12] some SDS chapters come closer to qualifying as subversive conspiracies than others. The movement as a whole does not, as yet. Nevertheless, a fatal mistake was made in embracing the open membership policy in the first place. Every experience with "the openings to the left" in Europe or America has shown that those who come into a loose association or federation as disciplined masters of parliamentary tactics, and with an ideology expressed in secret caucuses and hidden agenda, will sooner or later rule or ruin the general movement. That is precisely what is now happening as the original spontaneity of the new left yields to ideological discipline and harsh attempts to tear down the college and university and the style of life they have for so long represented.[13]

Thunder on the Right

Although the threat of the left should not be underestimated, especially on the campuses and in the civil rights and peace movements, the most dangerous internal challenge to America comes from the fascist wing. The amount of heavy financing centered in the John

[12] See Chapters II and III on the Totalitarianism "Grid."

[13] The writer is obligated to Drs. Shoben and Wardell of the American Council on Education for a useful report on SDS history (May, 1968).

Birch Society and its "fronts" has grown from $1 million in 1961 to between $46 million and $50 million in 1968. Distinct from honest conservatism, which accepts orderly and wise change as both natural and desirable, fascism is nihilistic, power-hungry, and revolutionary in both theory and tactics. Driven by a closed system of secret truths, known only to the elite, the pathological right has opted out of the public dialogue and speaks only in a shrill monologue to those outside the sound-proof room.

When in the minority, the genuine conservative builds a "loyal opposition." A loyal opposition participates vigorously in the public debate, improving its quality and sometimes changing its direction. A loyal opposition stays within the "rules of the game," having confidence in the basic integrity of the constitutional order and the power of full, free, and informed discussion to correct error. A loyal opposition, when out of office, proposes specific alternatives and builds a "shadow cabinet" so that the electorate may be clear on the choices involved. The pseudo-conservative follows the lead of the demagogues, with a frenzy of unrestrained attacks on public policy and a minimal offering of constructive alternative proposals. Regarding the public debate as meaningless, the totalitarian demagogue is only present to evangelize his own ideology—never to learn. Tearing and rending public confidence in the Constitution (and Bill of Rights!) where he can, his style is conspiracy, and his stench is disloyalty. The pseudo-conservative is the "patsy," the fellow traveler to the fascists; the genuine conservative is their mortal enemy.

The genuine conservative accepts the need for gradual change and tries to bring it about in a way that preserves treasured values; the pseudo-conservative holds the line against change until explosive, revolutionary force has built up which can be used to concretize his ideology. The genuine conservative is loyal to the Constitution and due process of law; he is equally opposed to betrayal of law and order by the police or other public officials and to violence by mobs. The pseudo-conservative praises police power and treats the rights of ordinary citizens with contempt. The true conservative judges politics by the human measure; the pseudo-conservative will destroy a city, a nation, or a world for the sake of slogans and abstract propositions. The true conservative believes "that people, in the last analysis, are the best judges of their own interests." [14] Aware that the public dialogue includes fathers and fathers' fathers as well as those present, he only insists that the decision-making process shall not—through haste and excessive zeal—neglect the dialogue with the past. The pseudo-conservative asserts that "democracy . . . is a perennial fraud" [15] and in his posture of patron of the people respects neither the historical background to constitutional self-government nor the present imperfect alternatives confronting the citizenry. The John Birch Society, a disciplined party of pseudo-conservatives and fascists, is a dangerous threat to both sound politics and high religion.

On the political front it is the ardent defender of police-state measures against religious dissent, campus dissent, and political opposition—where it thinks to muster support against unpopular minorities—and it is

[14] Murray Clark Havens, *The Challenges to Democracy* (Austin: Univ. of Texas Press, 1965), p. 10.
[15] Robert Welch. *The Blue Book* (Boston: privately printed, 1959), p. 159.

the eager exponent of defiance of the law where polarizing seems a power-building strategy. What is needed in
America is not a fascist adventure but a national ally,
a gathering up of the forces of unity and cohesion—as
President Nixon rightly sounded the call in his inaugu-
ral address. But to achieve that we must strengthen
the middle ground of dialogue and rub off the lustre
and the fascination from the rule-or-ruin approach. To
the young and impatient especially, the all-or-nothing
attitude in poltitics has distinct appeal. The willingness
to compromise and to accept proximate solutions and
limited objectives comes later in life, if the person ma-
tures. Pathological politics, with its panoply of surface
glory—from the ecstatic language of demagogues to the
colorful shirts of the fascist and Communist elite—is
the politics of continued adolescence. It is also the
language of "the final conflict"—enthusiastically proclaimed and eagerly sought after.

Which America?

Some months ago the Senate Permanent Subcommit-
tee on Investigations was holding a hearing on the
causes of the Detroit uprising in 1967. Listening were
Senators John L. McClellan, Democrat of Arkansas,
and Carl T. Curtis, Republican of Nebraska, the only
members in attendance. In spite of the testimony of
leading churchmen and security specialists like J. Edgar
Hoover, who have all agreed that the 1967 outbursts
were uncoordinated acts of desperation, the senators
were ardently pursuing the red herring of the radical
right: that a conspiracy was the cause of it all, and that
sterner police measures should be taken against mobs.

The witness was George Romney, then Republican governor of Michigan. "We must be quick to keep the peace," he said. "But we must be just as quick to strike down the denials of basic human justice which encourage violence and disorder. For we cannot expect to have law and order without justice." While the two self-styled conservatives listened in silence, the Governor went on to issue a conservative warning. He said it would be possible to pass suppressive legislation and leave the questions of human dignity, job opportunity, and decent education untouched; but then, he said prophetically, "our system would become little better than a police state." [16]

Mr. Romney was quite right, and by implication he drew the line at the right place. The issue today falls between those with hope in America—those who are determined to expand this glorious experiment in liberty and self-government to benefit all American citizens—and those who have decided to hold the line for old injustices and wickedness and to destroy the Bill of Rights itself, if necessary, to keep things the way they think they once were. The night air is full of extremist voices calling Americans "back to the good old days." The halls of our legislatures are full of voices trying to hold back the future of the American people, *all* of our citizens—some of them defying laws and constitutional rights of citizens that have been on the books for a full century. I am ashamed to say that in a recent major test of justice versus special privilege, the Civil Rights Act of 1968, both senators from Iowa voted on the wrong side.

The issue is a far larger one than racial justice, however. It is even larger than the question of whether a

[16] *The New York Times*, 3/20/68, p. 28.

world that is 80 percent colored will tolerate much longer an America which talks with a forked tongue. The argument that we must practice decent human relations for the sake of our international "image" is, after all, a self-serving one. The issue is whether human liberty and self-government are to succeed and to expand on the face of the earth, or whether despotism and police state practices are to come to triumph. If the latter happens, no group will bear a larger responsibility than the congressmen themselves—eager as some of them may be to pass the blame off on the blacks and poor whites of the ghetto and the alienated youth and students of the age of the atom bomb. A Congress which, in a world of starvation (including 35 million Americans), can spend $159 billion a year for the military and only $8 billion for economic aid (domestic and foreign) has, among many of the young, lost its claim to credibility as an agency of decision-making.

If the American experiment goes down, it makes little difference whether the demise is a triumph of fascist, Communist, racist, or national socialist politics. Those who love liberty want the success of neither a Stokely Carmichael, who was "playing the Lenin game" in Washington the summer of 1968, nor a Robert Welch, whose disciplined political troops are even now urging police state measures from local to national level. The Bircher slogan for the season of despair and desperation is "Support Your Local Police"—and what kind of sadistic police behavior they have in mind is evident from the fact that they have been sponsoring former Sheriff Jim Clarke of Selma, Alabama, on speaking tours across the country. Clarke's chief claim to fame is that he used cattle prods on American citizens. One of the most awful figures of the twentieth century is the lawless policeman!

The far more dangerous political weapon to which the fascists are turning is, however, the effort to destroy public confidence in our Constitution, the courts, and our Chief Executive. To accomplish this goal, they must tear down confidence in the ability of the people to govern themselves and in the integrity of our national leadership. The assault on Chief Justice Earl Warren is long-standing. The lying assault on the church and synagogue and university leaders has gone on for years. The defamation of the Chief Executive—Eisenhower, Kennedy, Johnson, and now Nixon—is constant. Recent monthly bulletins of the John Birch Society have charged that both sides in Vietnam are controlled by the same "insiders"—i.e., the Jews—that President Johnson deliberately sacrificed American boys in Vietnam to further the Communist goals, that President Nixon also is a tool, and that the governments in Moscow and Washington cooperate like two arms of the same body.

At the same time, the occult explanation for the bad military situation in Southeast Asia is that the military leadership is being betrayed at home—by the civilian control of the military arm, and by those who are struggling for civil rights and justice in our cities. I personally believe that Dr. Martin Luther King, Jr., made a serious mistake in linking the civil rights issue to the peace issue, but the fascists are trying to forge that link with their own version of the "stab-in-the-back" theory.

It should be noted that one of the myths which contributed most to the rise of fascism and Nazism was the "stab-in-the-back" theory: Mussolini told the young veterans that the liberals and socialists had robbed Italy of the spoils of victory. Hitler and the German generals told the people Germany was defeated because the liberals and socialists injected social revolution at home while brave German soldiers were winning on the battlefields. Today the well-poisoners in America, notably the John Birch Society and fellow travelers, are trying to fabricate the myth that American arms would have been victorious in Asia but for the "liberal" and "socialist" and "Communist" demonstrations in our cities.

The "stab-in-the-back" theory is a fabrication, fostered by incompetents to hide their own betrayal of the people. The painful truth is that the President of the United States has been wretchedly ill-advised by his generals and his intelligence services. They have had tens of billions of dollars of the taxpayers' money to work with. They started with the virtually unanimous desire of the American people to stop the spread of communism in Southeast Asia. They have had several hundred thousand young Americans drafted into uniforms and sent to distant places to implement their plans. And with all this, the generals have proved incapable of effecting their mission, and the intelligence services have shown themselves wildly incompetent to predict percentages in effectiveness of policy. The American soldier has fought valiantly; his superiors have shown themselves extraordinarily inept. They have consistently failed in their predictions and their promises, and the Commander-in-Chief finally found that he had led the American people into a major undeclared war in Asia—something against which every wise military mind has warned for years—because of the unreliability of his military advisers.

If anybody has been "stabbed in the back," it is the long-suffering American people, who—like the Italian and German people years ago—have sacrificed their sons and daughters' lives and happiness on a prodigious scale, only to have their trust betrayed by military and intelligence officials incompetent in military and intelligence matters.

In the meantime those who have placed their bets on national disaster are carefully laying the basis for a *coup d'état* in their fascist-type literature, charging that the fault lies not with those who have had virtually all our power and all our money tied up for years in Vietnam, but with the "liberals, socialists and com-symps" who are trying to get a little attention given to our rat-ridden cities, sewage-poisoned rivers, cockroach-infested tenements, and crowded schoolrooms.

The truth is, of course, that the battle for liberty is indivisible—and we cannot save and strengthen the cause of self-government by turning over power to the fascists at home or by appeasing the Communists abroad. There is a wise saying from an English political scientist of another generation: "You can peel an onion skin by skin, but you cannot skin a tiger paw by paw. His business is vivisection, and he'll get you first." The encounter with totalitarian ideologies, parties, and systems is a meeting with flesh-eaters, as anyone who has been involved in it knows. Over a place of meeting —whether in a trade union local, a student caucus, or at Berlin—the question has been written large by a leading Communist theoretician (Lenin): "Who? whom?" And their favorite weapon against the rising tide of human persons' awareness of their dignity and liberty—as good Pope John put it—is, wherever they can subvert officials or capture government, to hurl lawless police action against the citizens.

The John Birch Society is not to be considered a political education organization: it is a "body," [17] that is, it is a totalitarian political party, seeking power. The

[17] *The Blue Book*, p. 109.

reversion from *Gesellschaft* (a complex of rationally constructed and balanced constitutional procedures) to *Gemeinschaft* (a personal, familial entity of primary and unreflective relationships) is typical of totalitarian movements of the fascist type. The attempt is made to turn back from modern, sophisticated, specialized structures—where a pluralism of powers and sovereignties makes all political solutions ambiguous and imperfect—to the simple procedures of the tribe led by a—perchance benevolent—patriarch.

The implacable hostility of the John Birch Society to constitutions, bills of rights, and due process of law is not accidental therefore. Neither is it tactical, reflecting "tough" politics. It is grounded in the contempt which the primitivist feels for all sophistications, all historical compromises, all developed structures. It pretends an upward gage, but its path leads downward into the abyss.

According to the Bible, hell is the place where those who have power misuse it—not to protect the defenseless, but to torment the helpless. This is precisely what hell is, politically speaking—whether we glimpse its red flames in Sharpesville, South Africa, Orangeburg, South Carolina, or Waterloo, Iowa.

The question is not just degenerate politics, somewhat disagreeable for Christians to discuss anyhow. The question is the countenance of the age. The ultimate question deals with salvation itself.

A Substitute Religion

Dr. J. A. Broyles is quite correct in identifying the John Birch Society as a substitute church—in the same

sense as the Nazi or Communist party—and its creed
as a substitute religion:

> The Birch Society and its leader serve both as func-
> tional alternatives to the church and to its Lord.
> Religion has come to be something that they can use
> for their own purpose rather than a relationship to a
> God who uses them for His purposes.[18]

The attempt of John Birch Society fascists to use organized religion, which has tormented so many congregations across the country in recent years, reveals the
deeper loyalty: to the *Weltanschauung* and the discipline of a totalitarian sect. Hans Buchheim analyzed
the phenomenon of substitute religions in the Third
Reich very ably, in *Glaubenskrise im Dritten Reich*
(Stuttgart, 1953). Analysis of the eschatology, anthropology and soteriology of the John Birch Society shows
striking parallels to the Nazi party. For the true believer it is a faith substitute; for the ordinary follower,
the cultic symbols and rites suffice.

As Welch says, the first chapter of *The Blue Book*
ends on "quite a religious note." [19] A cosmic battle, a
modern presentation of the ancient Zoroastrian cosmo-
logical struggle between the forces of light and darkness, is joined. The Communists are "those beasts" and
Welch himself is "a man on a white horse." [20] The
present age is controlled by the forces of evil, with our
own government the most powerful enemy.[21]

[18] J. A. Broyles, *The John Birch Society* (Boston: Beacon
Press, 1964), p. 122.
[19] *The Blue Book*, p. 38.
[20] *The Blue Book*, p. 76.
[21] *The Blue Book*, p. 32. Robert Welch, *The Politician* (Boston, Belmont Publishing Co., 1964), p. 5. President Eisenhower,
according to Welch, was "completely controlled" by the Communists (p. 6), planted in the presidency by the Communists
to "throw the game" (p. 133).

Man in general is inspired by an "upward reach" [22] of unending potential. His passionate errors are simply "an unfortunate weakness." But man in particular is treated with loathing contempt: only words such as "slimy," "slick," "cheap," and "unsavory" can describe him.

The Blue Book, although its author scarcely perceived what he was revealing of his own disloyalty to historic religion, is explicit enough:

> Far from founding a religion, we are merely urging Protestants, Catholics, Jews, or Moslems to be better Christians, better Jews, or better Moslems, in accordance with the deepest and most humanitarian promptings of their own religious beliefs. And we are simply trying to draw a circle of faith in God's power and purpose, and of man's relationship to both, which is broad and inclusive enough to take each man's specific faith into that circle without violation. Yet the evangelical fervor, with which we expect our members to fight the forces of evil and work for a better world, makes certain principles with regard to religious groups apply to ourselves. [23]

Sometimes the remoteness of the unknown God yields to another doctrine, equally heretical. Taylor Caldwell, the literary darling of the radical right, declared with the fervor of the Zuickau prophets of the sixteenth century:

> Let your clergy tell you that your place is in the streets shouting, but know that your "place" is in eternity and not in this world. How do I know these things? Not only from great and humble pastors in my early life, but from . . . a personal revelation. [24]

[22] *The Blue Book,* pp. 149ff.

[23] *The Blue Book,* p. 168.

[24] Taylor Caldwell, "Where Are Our Shepherds?" *American Opinion* (Feb., 1968), p. 96.

Caldwell—like Welch, no trained theologian—makes the typical low-grade confusion of the gods of place and the gods of time. "Eternity" and "world" are *not places* in the New Testament, although they are in the philosophies of the heathen: they are *ages* (eons). And the one who does not in this life devote himself to peace, justice, and righteousness will—in the age to come—inherit damnation. This includes Taylor Caldwell, however assiduously he may in this life cultivate the pose of a self-taught stoic. No one who has read Isaiah or Amos or Hosiah could say that "civil rights is a purely spiritual matter" [25]—although the pseudo-intellectual who strains after the spirit of Marcus Aurelius can.

Finally, in spite of his appeals to "Christian America" and general addiction to an ethnic perversion of "religion," Welch's basic atheism is evident:

> It is hard for man to realize that the Infinite still remains infinite, untouched in Its remoteness and unreduced in Its infinity by man's most ambitious approaches; or that all of man's increasing knowledge leaves the Unknowable just as completely unknowable as before. But I think that, being allowed now to grasp this truth, we should cease to quarrel and disagree over how close we are to God. For we are using a term which, in a literal context, or objectively, has no meaning.[26]

The advocates of the "death of God" theology, never put it more plainly: "God" has no objective or real meaning. But whereas Bishop John Robinson and William Hamilton turned to service of the compassionate Jesus, much as the medieval mystics relieved

[25] Taylor Caldwell, "Not Cricket," *American Opinion* (March 1968), p. 23.
[26] *The Blue Book*, p. 147.

peal. Honest conservatives, in the church as well as in the body politic, know the difference between loyal opposition and its counterfeit. One of the most important lessons for Christians of every viewpoint is to learn carefully to distinguish between informed dissent and the deliberate smear. The November 18 ad belongs in the latter category and falls outside the limits of the dialogue.

The Fellow Traveler

Whisking about the edges of any totalitarian movement is the "fellow traveler," pirouetting into the whirlpool and out again as the vortex draws more powerfully and then recedes. His role is as dangerous to social health and as important to building up totalitarian parties as the equally ambiguous figure of the pseudo-conservative. The fellow traveler to the Communists or fascists is a fascinating psychological study: fascination with brute force and its misuse plays an important role. Students of communism have commented at length upon the party member's "psychology of the pawn"—his need to be misused and abused, to the destruction of his own personhood. The fellow traveler's responses are essentially feminine, registering the ambivalence of love and hate toward the master and mover.

The fellow traveler refuses to accept discipline and is therefore both used and despised by the party leaders. At the same time, he is dangerous to political movements and republican institutions of integrity, because he functions as a deceiver. He appears at times to be independent, but, when a major issue is at stake, he follows the party line.

Perhaps the most famous type in recent years was Von Ribbentrop, pseudo-intellectual and champagne salesman, who was of great use to the Nazi government in giving an aura of respectability to international policies which, without a debonair front, might have been recognized readily for what they were: simple thuggery.

In America, the outstanding representative of this function is William F. Buckley, Jr., editor of *The National Review* and perennial political candidate. Buckley got his start as a smart young "intellectual" by writing a book, *God and Man at Yale*, upon graduating from his *alma mater*. The book has been soundly exposed and condemned by professors and overseers and loyal alumni for falsely twisting facts and for sheer malice. *The National Review* and his syndicated newspaper column, "On the Right," frequently print "news items" and interpretations picked up from the openly fascist journals and have been important and useful agencies for radical right attacks on honest liberals and conservatives.

Buckley has been caught out for misquotations (with quotation marks!) and for repeating radical right malice and rumor, but he never admits a mistake or apologizes to the victims. Like Westbrook Pegler, who lied day after day in his column about Quentin Reynolds and goaded him into a lawsuit, Buckley could be taken to court by any one of several people who had enough money to hire competent legal counsel and nothing else to do. Reynolds won his suit, of course, but it took all of his time and resources for most of three years, and he died shortly thereafter.

As his lack of respect for the rules of the dialogue and his constant undermining of respect for American leadership and institutions reveal, Buckley is not a "conservative" at all. The streak of ideological taint and moral nihilism is too pronounced, even though he is probably not under the direct control of any subversive party. When he publicly criticized Robert Welch of the John Birch Society, Buckley did not do it because Welch led a fascist-type conspiracy and used immoral tactics to undermine the constitutional order. Buckley said Welch was too extreme to be successful. When Dr. Martin Luther King, Jr. was assassinated, Buckley wrote in his column a tortuously reasoned explanation that the murderer represented the error of an independent conscience, which was Dr. King's error too.

"Truth," asked Pilate, "What is truth?"

The Fascist International

We have been concerned to portray the dangers to America, her politics, and her religions, but the international scope of fascism should never be ignored. The Communist International is so much better financed and so impressively effective at times that we are apt to forget that there is also a radical right international. The activities of the so-called International Council of Christian Churches attracts newspaper attention from time to time, holding rump sessions, as it does on occasion, to try to embarrass assemblies of the World Council of Churches.

The connections are more precise yet, however. Not long ago I received a letter from a high-ranking British officer with whom I worked for years in the British and American zones of occupation in postwar Germany. He is now living in Rhodesia and wrote: "What do you know of an 'anti-communist' chap named Hargis, or something like that? He appeared on our TV, claimed that he was invited to Rhodesia by Ian Smith and will conduct lectures here in January, 1970. . . . I thought he was clever in a way I dislike—half a story, an illogical deduction, and thus a 'proof.' He really is not worth writing about, but our authorities seem to sponsor that sort of character."

An even more dramatic evidence of radical right collaboration across national lines came to the surface in precise detail in the Naudé and Geyser libel suit against Pont in South Africa. In one of the most important civil suits of this century, two Dutch Reformed theologians, Professor A. S. Geyser of the University of Witwatersrand and Reverend C. F. Beyers Naudé, head of the Christian Institute of South Africa, brought a libel suit against Professor A. D. Pont, who teaches church history at the predominantly Afrikaans-speaking Pretoria University.

The plaintiffs charged that articles by Professor Pont, appearing in the official Dutch Reformed journal *Die Hervormer* in late 1964 and early 1965, constituted defamation of character because they stated that the several ecumenical conferences that Professor Geyser and the Reverend Mr. Naudé attended were sponsored by the World Council of Churches and were for the purpose of providing a way for the WCC to promote "Pan-Africanism." Pont also leveled charges that, because Geyser and Naudé attended these meetings, they were "traitors and tools of international communism." Pont also attacked the Christian Institute, which is the main center of the ecumenical movement in South Africa, as a medium being used to bring "leftist" and "Communist" ideas into the South African churches. Pont attacked especially the emphasis placed on multiracial seminars and the Christian Institute's position that Article 3 of the NHK (Nederduits Hervermde Kerk) Church, which excluded all non-whites from church membership, was not in keeping with scripture. Pont stated that "multi-racialism is a starting point (premise) of communism, which it propagates." [28] Another article written by Pont charged that "certain South African theologians" (namely, Geyser and Beyers Naudé) were out to overthrow the existing government of South Africa. "The suit charged that from the articles it could reasonably be assumed that those theologians were not only supporters of communism, sabotage, and revolution, but were men of despicable moral character, were heretics and supporters of murder." [29]

In the outcome of the case, the plaintiffs won. Mr. Justice Trollip of the Rand Supreme Court awarded damages at the amount of $14,000 plus costs to each of the plaintiffs, the largest libel award ever granted in the history of South Africa.

In his report, Mr. Justice Trollip chastised Professor Pont for defamatory statements which could not be proved, for relying on second-hand information, for distorting conference reports to serve his own cause, for reckless charges against individuals with whom he did not agree, and for repeating charges he personally knew to be false.

It is yet too early to indicate the ramifications which this case might have for South Africa. However, there are some clear signs: (1) South Africa has begun to

[28] "Libel Action by Prof. A. S. Geyser and the Rev. Beyers Naudé vs. Prof. A. D. Pont," National Council of Churches: Department of Information *Report* No. X, p. 1.
[29] *The Christian Century*, March 15, 1967, p. 357.

build a body of law to deal with extremism. Even though this is a slight beginning, and the case was only a libel suit, it was certainly not a feeble beginning. It dealt squarely with the issue of careless attacks upon honest and fair-minded citizens.

(2) It was a crushing blow to the radical right in South Africa. Even though Professor Pont will be a martyr to some, the trial—especially the cross-examination by Attorney G. A. Coetzee—exposed the unethical methods used by Pont to discredit publicly those with whom he differed concerning the doctrine of the church. It should be remembered that Pont is a member of the Hertzog Group, an extreme group based on the totalitarian "Broederbund" and active in the South African apartheid government. Professor Pont is also a member of the "National Council to Combat Communism," and, in this council, he relies heavily on the leadership and advice of the Reverend Dr. J. G. Vorster, chairman of the council. Vorster is a brother of the prime minister and is also a powerful leader in the Hertzog Group. He has recently returned home from a visit to the United States, made on invitation by Edgar Bundy of the Church League of America.

(3) In preparing his attack and defense, Professor Pont drew upon a large list of American extremists' writings, including articles by Edgar Bundy and Billy James Hargis—leaders of right-wing organizations in this country. His group has also sponsored Bundy as a speaker in so-called "anti-Communist seminars" in South Africa, seminars in which Bundy has been even more reckless in charging American church leaders with being Communists than in his work as a spiritual bushwhacker in the United States.

Bundy and Hargis were, in spirit, on trial also. Views

and methods similar to theirs were found to be reckless, extreme, and irresponsible.

The Rand Supreme Court decision is a hopeful sign for freedom for all those who dwell under a totalitarian system or are fighting totalitarian movements elsewhere. This is one time when this country can find a model in South African justice, in how to deal with persons who spread vicious rumors destroying trust in church and elected officials, attempting to undermine the rule of law.[30]

In Rhodesia and South Africa, of course, government is in the hands of radical right racists. Those now ruling South Africa were, in fact, openly sympathetic to Hitler and his racist ideology. What then is the political and religious level of persons who, enjoying the privileges of American citizenship, travel abroad to serve the interests of such regimes? The records of their activity show clearly that they are hired to tell widely and often two big lies: one, that the civil rights movement in America is a Communist conspiracy and, two, that the National Council of Churches and its leaders are agents of a Communist conspiracy. They have no other function than that and, except for that, they would be uninteresting to those in control of the police states of Rhodesia and South Africa.

Since almost the only spiritual support given true Christians and champions of justice and due process of law in those areas comes from the ecumenical movement, the function of Hargis and Bundy as false proph-

---

[30] For detailed information see: "Libel Action by Prof. A. S. Geyser and the Rev. Beyers Naudé vs. Prof. A. D. Pont," National Council of Churches: Department of Information *Reports* I–XXIV, and *The Christian Century* for March 15, 1967; May 24, 1967; June 28, 1967; July 19, 1967.

ets is the same across the water as it is here: to try to sow discord among brethren. Nevertheless, it seems much more cowardly and unclean to lie about American church leaders in a foreign land and for foreign pay!

The international network of right-wing groups has been tragically demonstrated recently in Northern Ireland, where McIntire's agent, the "Reverend" Ian Paisley, has played upon ancient prejudice to organize violence against the Catholic minority. On Saturday, January 4, a particularly savage mob action was mobilized. At Londonderry a Catholic civil rights march pledged to nonviolence was ambushed by Protestant extremists wielding rocks, clubs, and even a Molotov cocktail. The police, who had a difficult day, were pledged to defend the constitutional liberties of the peaceful demonstrators and turned fire hoses against Paisley's mob. Whether or not the Catholics were right in feeling that they were being discriminated against in housing and jobs, they had the right peaceably to assemble and to march.[31]

In this country Protestant bigots of Paisly and McIntire stripe have ambused black citizens and attempted further to capitalize on racial antagonisms to mount their drive for political power. Unfortunately, in the Deep South the police have all too often joined the illegal mobs in attempting to crush groups of citizens exercising their rights as citizens.

The important thing to remember about the extremists, whether in Northern Ireland, America, or elsewhere, is that their slogan of "law and order" is a fraud. Disloyal to fair play in politics and indecent in their misuse of religion, they will turn to mob violence

[31] *Reuters* reports, 1/5/69 and 1/6/69.

the moment they find it to their advantage. Those who have no respect for the moral law are no safe champions of any laws. Those who use the language of religion to disguise a basic atheism of belief and action are what the Bible calls false prophets.

II

-•-•-•-•-

How to Identify
Totalitarian Movements

•-

ALTHOUGH the terms "extremism" and "radical right"
are widely used, they lack precision. So do "comsymp,"
"pink," and "new left." We shall continue to use them
on occasion to save time and to avoid endless repeti-
tion of the same word, but the malaise with which we
are dealing is specific, objectively definable. That problem is the rise of disciplined conspiratorial movements
whose goal is power and whose style of politics is contrary to the rule of liberty under law which republican
constitutions and due process of law are designed to
achieve.

Limited Use of the Term "Extremism"

The term "extremism" carries the implication that
the basic problem is one of intensity of opinion—as

though a person of mediocre views and lukewarm opinions were preferable to one of sturdy convictions. This is manifestly not the case, certainly not for Christians. The issue in the rise of Communist- and fascist-type parties is precisely that the ill-trained and half-formed baptized tend to be swept away, whereas genuine "confessing Christians" would stand fast to the truth. It is not intensity of opinions we are talking about, but the truth itself. The totalitarian world views are false, and the fact that they are often proclaimed by vehement minorities is secondary. So too with the term "radical right": the phrase is preferred by some writers who do not want to apply the precise rubric, which is fascism. "Fascism" was the term chosen by the oldest movement of right-wing take-over, when Mussolini and his thugs betrayed the legitimate goverment of Italy in 1922, terrorized and destroyed all dissenting groups, and established the model followed with adaptations by Hitler, Franco, Perón, and a host of subsequent lesser lights. "Fascism" is the term to apply to parallel movements and systems today, even though specialists note technical differences between Italian fascism, German Nazism, Spanish Falangism, and other radical right movements.

Again, from a technical point of view, there are differences in the communism of Lenin, Stalin, Khrushchev, Kosygin, and Tito, not to mention Mao and Ho; and there are differences between Communist systems operative today and the kind that Karl Marx and Friedrich Engels predicted. Some of these differences—for example, between the "national communism" of Yugoslavia and the world revolutionary thrust of Red China—may have very substantial effect upon world affairs. Since we are working with limited space and for lay readers, however, and especially because our task is a very specific one—to present the identifying marks of totalitarianism *per se*—we shall not attempt to distinguish in detail between the various elements of Communist thought such as "Marxism," "dialectical materialism," or "economic determinism."

The Ideological Taint

It is of the utmost importance to point up the difference between ideological politics of any kind, which short-circuit reasonable discussion with catch phrases and emotion-laden slogans, and the kind of pragmatic, prudent, problem-solving politics which is the genius of the English and American constitutional development. We would do well to divest ourselves of all sloganizing substitutes for intelligent dissension, including "capitalism," "private initiative," and defending "Christian America," to get down to the real business of politics—which is not to bring in the Kingdom, but to make organized life more livable. Even though they are not conspiracies, a substantial contribution to the last century of European political misery has been made by so-called Christian parties, which, with the Communists and fascists, helped to sloganize political decisions, polarize peoples, and corrupt both church and state.

This is the reason why the extremists' demand that Americans choose between "liberalism" (read: "soft on communism") and "conservatism" (read: "soft on fascism") is itself unhealthy. As a matter of fact, nothing is more critical than correcting the common error of referring to Communists as "progressive" and fascists as "conservative"; neither adjective is accurate.

Neither is it desirable to turn the Democratic party into a "liberal" party and the Republican party into a "conservative" party, although this is urged so vehemently by some well-meaning people as well as by all Communists and fascists. It is precisely the genius of the common law that ideological logic is avoided and the human measure retained. Most Americans are still, thank God, "liberal" on one issue and "conservative" on another, and most of us resent the insistence by the ideologically tainted that we be ideologically consistent. For those who try to live with man as the measure and who honor the dignity and liberty and integrity of the human person above all systems and institutions, this demand is not only improper, it is unclean, and it reveals the extent to which corrupting ideologies have affected even otherwise reasonable men.

The question is not whether the TVA is "socialist" and a private utility "capitalist"; the question for sensible people is how to get the cheapest electricity to the largest number of people. The question is not whether the government's post office department is "socialist" and the old pony express "private initiative"; the question for prudent people is how to get a cheap and efficient delivery of mail. The question is not whether public universities are "socialist" and private colleges are "capitalistic"; the question is how to get adequate and healthy higher education for American youth. In this case the strongest case can be made for a two-track system, and strong argument for a "mixed economy" of private and public sectors can be argued elsewhere as fitting the American system of checks and balances. But, in any case, let each issue be settled on its merits, with a minimum of sloganizing and ideological posturing.

The most difficult of all typological questions right now is how to view certain new organizations neither Communist nor fascist but manifestly a threat to the public opinion. In the case of black militants like RAM, the connection with Castroite communism seems fairly obvious. But what of the Black Muslims, who qualify as extremists in several respects but cannot be regarded as totalitarian in the full sense as long as they are apolitical, eschewing political power? "Strangers in the land" are not subversives and do not constitute a threat, even if their internal structure is highly authoritarian. How shall we view the Mafia, which has most of the characteristics of a conspiracy and yet it primarily aimed at economic aggrandizement? Now that the extent to which the Mafia has corrupted certain city machines, police forces, and municipal courts is increasingly clear, the need for civil action and legislation to put the totalitarian conspiracies out of business may become more evident. In such case, the question of whether an assault on the constitutional order is more "Communist" or more "fascist" is largely theoretical. Some of the most notorious totalitarian governments in the world, like several in the Arab League, gained power and operate internally as fascist juntas, while in foreign affairs they jump to do the bidding of their Russian allies.

To the loyal American trying to save his peace committee from being captured by a Communist cadre or his PTA from being taken over by a John Birch cell, the verbal niceties create a distinction without a difference. He can find comfort in the wisdom of an old Hutterite elder, chairman of a colony of simple, Bible-believing Christians in Montana. A visiting scholar was trying to discuss with him the role of the Christian in politics, a role which the Hutterites have shunned since their founding in 1528. (The conversation was all in German.) The visitor argued that in a republic the responsibility of citizens was different from that under the old absolute monarchs who ruled by divine right.

> Visitor: Do you pay taxes?
> H: Yes, we pay taxes.
> Visitor: Do you vote?
> H: No, we don't vote.
> Visitor: Why not, since you have the rights and protection of a republican form of government?
> H: Well, the Republicans and the Democrats are evenly divided in this county. If we voted, we'd talk it over beforehand and all vote the same. Then the loser would blame us.
> Visitor: But you know there are governments that persecute the Christians today, and even here in America there are people who attack the churches and the leaders of our country. Right here in the county seat town there are two John Birch cells. Do you know of the John Birchers?
> H: Yes, we know them.
> Visitor: What do you think of them?
> H: They're Communists.
> Visitor: Why do you say that?
> H: You can tell by the way they talk about the government.

Of course, the specialist might want to argue distinctions with the old gentleman, but with such instincts he won't go far wrong! Further, the totalitarianism "grid" [1] shows quite clearly that in terms of social pathology, as also revealed by a half-century of encounters with various conspiracies, the overlay between Communist and fascist types occurs at fourteen out of fifteen points. The "grid" affords a tool for identifying

[1] *Infra*, p. 72.

organizations and parties and systems which have opted out of the life of dialogue, which are not in good faith in public meetings, and have in fact drawn the knife against all who stand in the way of their drive for power.

The Special Responsibility of Academics and Churchmen

Teachers and preachers, and the faculties and congregations who look to them for leadership, have a built-in tendency to slight the importance of power structures and law in human affairs. Their own professions tend to maximize informal and interpersonal relations and to avoid tests of brute strength. Moreover, they are specialists in the use of words, and themselves were taught to believe that solving issues by discussion is a higher ethos than solving them with drawn knife. They have found it hard to face the fact that the totalitarians represent a throwback to more elemental encounter and that they must be dealt with at once if a maximum of nonviolent solution is to be achieved.

There was a time in the history of the Weimar Republic when just a few hundred preachers and teachers could have saved the constitution and reduced the Communists (KPD) and fascists (NSDAP) to ineffectiveness. They waited tentatively, however, convinced that the best educated and most Christian people in the world (as they saw it) would never follow the demagogues who were polarizing the public opinion and destroying the middle ground of reasonable politics. They waited, objectively, until too late.

In our own country our universities and churches have delayed much too long in taking the extremist threat seriously. On the world map communism has made appalling gains—and within such countries as Italy, West Germany, Sweden, France, Great Britain, Canada, and the United States the Communists have scored high in successful conspiracy, subverision, and espionage. In our own country, a host of adventurers and witch doctors has rushed in to propose fascist "solutions." Since the learned articles and books of the specialists were never translated for ordinary lay use, and since the denominational publishing houses failed to provide the adult study units and Sunday school literature which might responsibly have handled the Christian-Communist encounter, millions of people read the only stuff available—the political pornography of Phyllis Schafly, John Stormer, H. L. Hunt, Carl McIntire, Billy James Hargis, Kent Courtney, and Edgar Bundy.

Reliable materials prepared by scholars with honest degrees and/or honorable ordinations are now available in sufficient quantity to supply the needs of the vast majority of thinking citizens and church people. It is a tribute to the common sense of the American people and to the loyalty of church members that, as acute as the issue obviously has been and as little responsible leadership as has been generally available, few have to date followed the fascist claim that they have the only answer to communism. Few Americans, in spite of the tens of millions of dollars used annually by the John Birch Society and its satellite organizations and "fronts," have been prepared to follow Robert Welch in the expressed conviction that Americans "can no longer resist the Communist conspiracy as free citizens,

but can resist the Communist conspiracy only by themselves becoming conspirators against established government." [2] Perhaps they remembered that Adolf Hitler came to power in Germany on two slogans: one,
restore law and order; two, save Europe from communism. More likely, like loyal Americans, they despised
both Communist and fascist conspiracies and subversives, and remained stubbornly determined not to be
drawn into the pressure area of either.

The critical and dependable materials are now available to analyze the challenge of totalitarianism as a
whole. Studies of totalitarianism now occupy a considerable section of the library shelves in any institution devoted to recent religious history or current
events in general. In a very real sense, the major motif
of the twentieth century is the struggle of Christianity
with alternative ideologies, and the encounter of the
open society with closed systems. Such studies are
chiefly found in monograph form, and where seminars
or institutes exist they are generally devoted to some
specialized phase of the problem—as at MIT, Harvard,
Columbia, UCLA, and Stanford. With the exception
of seminars at Santa Barbara, St. Louis University, and
Chicago Theological Seminary, there is no consistent
effort to study and interpret the phenomenon of totalitarianism as a whole.

Nevertheless, there is now enough material in hand
to make possible more intensive and consistent study,
among both professionals and lay students. The study,
since totalitarianism by definition involves all areas of
individual and social existence, affords a prime opportunity for interdisciplinary cooperation on campus. In
totalitarian parties and systems we encounter the end

[2] *The Blue Book*, p. 29.

of privacy, the most blessed privilege of civilized man. We also encounter the end of liberty for voluntary associations. Totalitarianism is like cancer, all-pervasive and covert, which affects every field from art and architecture to zoology. The study of totalitarianism affords a solid base for cooperative work, and in the present age—when the totalitarian threat is so pronounced—the style of study is inevitably that of action-research. So also among lay study groups, understanding of the totalitarian threat is inevitably action oriented.

The material now available is sufficient to make possible some generalizations concerning totalitarian ideologies, parties and systems. For example, the architecture of the Nazi *Haus der Kunst* in Munich and the Russian War Memorial in East Berlin has affinity if not identity. On the practical side, it is now perfectly possible to distinguish honest libralism from fellow-traveling with the Communists, and honest conservatism from fellow-traveling with fascist-type movements. The failure to make such distinction, scientifically as possible as the distinction between measles and scarlet fever, is the major plague afflicting both the Republican and Democratic parties in the United States. There is, of course, a distinction to be made between ideological parties seeking power and those that have won power and are operating governments. Yet the elaboration of a totalitarianism "grid" makes it possible to distinguish them all from the alternative styles and systems of politics. It can be objectively established that there is a fundamntal difference between fascist governments such as those of Greece and the Union of South Africa, or Communist goverments such as those of East Germany (D.D.R.) or China—although all claim to speak for "the people"—and authentic structures of liberty and representative government. The development of such a "grid" thus has both practical and theoretical importance.

Social Pathology

The study itself is social pathology. Just as in the field of medicine pathological studies illuminate the nature of healthy bodies, so the study of "sick societies" can illuminate the nature of social health. The thing which is sadly needed, the thing to which neither universities nor churches have given sufficient attention is the support of such study. One result is that in America today a vacuum exists between the national government's leaders, sworn to uphold the Constitution, and the wide variety of adventurers and witch doctors exploiting the anti-Communist racket for all it is worth. Another result is that an outstanding area of interdisciplinary research and publication has been neglected, even though there exist centers and departments and institutes in the universities on almost any other subject under the sun.

Even though there are obvious affinities, totalitarianism is quite different from the type of tyrannies and despotisms which for centuries afflicted human kind. As a study of the "grid" will disclose, the factors which make it possible are largely restricted to the twentieth century. There are contact points in native American culture, as there are in other peoples' tribal histories. Indeed, totalitarianism is in one sense a studied effort to return to the psychological and political womb of an earlier and simpler age. But only in the modern

period have self-contained and viable totalitarian systems come to the fore.

Totalitarianism presents a crisis of law, not just a
challenge of opinion. Without an adequate typological
approach, however, the legal rejoinder has been haphazard and inadequate. The nineteenth-century legal
philosophy, with its doctrines of popular revolution,
self-determination of peoples, and inalienable individual freedoms, has been unable to cope with the
Communist and fascist conspiracies and subversions.
There is a lack of understanding about what style of
group dissent builds up the public opinion and what
tears down representative government. Illinois has a
statute against racial defamation, Maryland has a law
against cross burning, and other minor measures exist.
West Germany was the only country that tried for a
time with considerable success to outlaw both Communist and fascist conspiracies. But the federal Congress has to date been unable to pass much legislation
which avoids the constitutional negatives to bills of
attainder and required self-incrimination. Congress,
heavily infiltrated by native fascists has not been able
to pass legislation which would outlaw the Ku Klux
Klan and the John Birch Society as well as the Communist party. Even though a recent case in the Union
of South Africa declared a heavy judgment for libel—
in the suit of Geyser and Naudé against Pont (an agent
of the radical right), the decisions of the Supreme
Court in this country have, by and large, protected
totalitarian individuals and associations rather than the
injured parties. The fact that such decisions were neces-
sitated by defective legislation simply underlines the
need to find a way out of the prevailing confusion.

Totalitarian movements face a difficult task, perhaps

an impossible one in a healthy society: to corrupt and undermine the oral tradition and constitutional order. In fact, they can only make real headway where the military has defected or where civil officers in government fail to keep their oaths of office. This is one compelling reason for voting down candidates for office who are ideologically tainted. But if it is true that an objective "grid" can be formulated, then there is a sound basis for constitutional legislation which will not leave the suppression and defeat of totalitarian thrusts solely to the "common sense" of the electorate. It is my contention that totalitarian conspiracies and actions can be defined by law as precisely as murder, arson, and rape, and that such definition is overdue.

One point must be made clear at the beginning: the "grid" can only be applied in the defense and strengthening of a society where liberty and self-government and constitutional processes still function. Where totalitarian rule already prevails, where defenders of the liberty and dignity and integrity of human persons are already in the underground, the rules no longer apply. In a revolutionary situation, or under foreign occupation, principles operative in a healthy order no longer apply. In short, under Communist or fascist government, resistance to prevailing laws may become a moral imperative for a lover of liberty.

In the following "grid" to define the totalitarian caucuses and systems, no one point is conclusive. If, however, a movement or system fits ten or twelve of these points, it is no longer part of the public debate, it is no longer of the nature of a loyal opposition, and the measures taken to combat it are of another level and another order from open debate or education. The issue becomes one of law: how much force, and of what kind, is necessary to put the flesh-eaters out of business? The earlier effective action is taken, the less violence will be necessary.

The Totalitarianism "Grid I" (Theoretical)

[1] ANTI-SEMITISM. Anti-Semitism is often the earliest and most certain seismographic reading on incipient totalitarianism. The attacks on the Jews and "the political churches" (*i.e.*, churches not reduced to family or tribal cults) is endemic to totalitarian movements and societies. The term "anti-Semitism" is actually inadequate and misleading, deriving from the presuppositions of an earlier humanitarian philosophy. Certain regimes run by racial Semites may fit one or more points on the "grid." The real issue is the totalitarian hostility to biblical history, to the Jewish contribution to civilization. The Teutons and pan-Slavs and Anglo-Saxons of totalitarian bent resent not Semites but the claim that history is carried and given its meaning by Israel. The defenders of German Christianity, of the Nazi *"positives Christentum,"* were theological liberals who had destroyed the authority of the Old Testament and repudiated the essential Jewishness of Christianity. In Christendom itself, which for centuries represented a compromise between biblical universalism and the tribal loyalties of western Europe, the basis for anti-Semitic policy was given in the decrees of the Fourth Lateran council in A.D. 1215; the ghetto for Jews was a necessary consequence.

The totalitarian ideology cannot, with its *Weltanschauung* and understanding of history, accept the truth that the only tribal history approved of God was Jewish. In the Bible, real history begins at Sinai. All other tribes of mankind enter history by being grafted on a Semitic tree, through the One who was of David's lineage.

Those Jews who suffered and perished in Hitler's Third Reich, and who suffer elsewhere today, suffer for the Lord of history—as would the Christians too if they did not betray their baptism and revert to their racial or tribal identity as gentiles. Where the Christians have remained faithful, they too have been attacked.

It is an error to discuss anti-Semitism in the same context as persecution of Arminians, American Indians, or Negroes. Racist policies are frequently related to the totalitarian longing for an earlier tribal homogeneity, and as such are inhumane. Racism is, to be sure, indecent and vulgar; anti-Semitism is blasphemous.

[2] IDEOLOGICAL POLITICS. Communists commonly interpret fascist dictatorship in economic terms such as "the triumph of the petit bourgeois." Fascists commonly interpret Communist dictatorship as "atheistic": that is, proponents of dialectical materialism deny the "supernatural" or "idealistic" order. Even in these phrases, however, both schools of thought reveal their own slavery to ideology. For the totalitarian, politics is part of a sacred science, a hidden wisdom known only to the initiates. For this reason the totalitarian cults have been rightly termed forms of "political Gnosticism," e.g., religion substitutes. Totalitarian politics is the politics of ultimates, with issues commonly stated in "god-terms." Politics is caught up by the closed mind into a closed system, to the displacement of all historic religions.

For the lover of liberty and self-government, however, politics is pragmatic, problem-solving, and prudent. It does not deal with the last things, but with present problems of the common life. Since Christianity has itself been misused as an ideology, especially in so-called Christian political parties and Christian trade unions, the basic issue is often obscured. In the American setting, there is an apparent affinity between the closed mind of fundamentalism (an ideological perversion of Christianity) and fascist-type politics. That such is not necessary, however, the German experience amply documents: there it was the conservatives and not the liberals who mounted the church struggle with Nazism.

For the Christian, politics will always bear the mark of the Fall, and political action will always be as limited, controlled, circumspect, modest—and carried on in as low a tone of voice as possible. Not so with Communists and fascists; in shrill voices and ecstatic utterances they preach their politics as the "science of the future." It is, above all, the ideological cast of totalitarianism which makes it a theological challenge.

[3] THE POLITICS OF POLARIZATION.   The rise of totalitarian parties has destroyed the politics of compromise and coalitions. The record is clear enough: whether in "united front" activities or in coalition governments (postwar Czechoslovakia? Poland? Vietnam?), the totalitarian bloc is never in good faith. In practice, the ideological mind-set can be recognized by its rule-or-ruin style of politics, which contrasts so markedly to the style of a loyal opposition. A loyal opposition, with an alternative plan of action and "shadow cabinet," is not only tolerable but necessary to liberty and self-government. The totalitarians, on the other hand, are

destructive of the rules of the dialogue and of the constitutional order itself. They intend not orderly change and transfer of power but reversion to the law of the knife.

The tactics of polarization are appealing sometimes even to pedestrian politicians. DeGaulle almost threw away a recent French election by attempting the destruction of the parties of the middle. The responsible action to strengthen self-government, however, is to build up the vital center. Liberals and conservatives have far more in common with each other than they have with Communist or fascist blocs. This is why "liberals" must avoid united fronts with Communists, and "conservatives" must shun coalition with John Birchers and others of fascist leaning.

[4] RECONSTRUCTION OF SACRAL SOCIETY. For the ideological mind, the "true believer," politics is not just a question of power: it is a religious issue. In sacral society, religious or ideological symbols control all aspects of organized life. Organismic and corporative theories of the state, a superpersonality, are proclaimed. (In the English constitutional tradition, "state" is a term rarely used; those holding office are called "the government," and the word of reference is "they," not "it.") Politics becomes Messianic, apocalyptic, at the same time that specific religious loyalties fade and die out. (The wild-eyed "little old ladies in tennis shoes," with their passion for final solutions, used to knit and raise money for foreign missions—where their devotion served a constructive purpose. Today their zeal is directed against Chief Justice Warren, the Fifth Amendment to the Constitution, and the councils and assemblies of the churches.) In our constitutional tradition,

enthusiasm is the business of the churches and a color-less common sense the style of government; in the to-talitarian scheme the roles are reversed. The fascist groups usually propose to return to a myth called "Christian America" (white, Anglo-Saxon, Protestant). The Communist groups propose to erect a new style of state church, of government use and misuse of ulti-mates. The Nazis were ambivalent between an artificial "German faith" and a use of the churches to recon-struct "Christendom" as a bulwark against Bolshevism.

To the one who loves liberty, the best government is "secular," that is, limited and—theologically speak-ing—"creaturely." It is a planned, rational, human in-vention to serve human ends. Religious liberty, which separates the religious covenants (the communities of ultimate truth) from the political covenant (the asso-ciation of proximate ends and transitory necessities), is to be reckoned one of the greatest gains in human history. The totalitarian attempt to return to "fellow-ship" (Gemeinschaft) in politics is rejected, along with the whole remythologizing process—whether of Chris-tendom or Marxism, "the Germanic folk-myth," or "the American religion."

The crime of the totalitarian systems is their disre-spect for the dignity and integrity and liberty of the human person and their brutal mistreatment of the person or group of dissenting conscience. We do right to be horrified by mob action in various parts of the free world, especially when it is permitted or sometimes even abetted by corrupt police forces. Far worse, how-ever, is the system in which the brutalization and de-humanization of individuals is a fixed policy of gov-ernment.

Communist and fascist systems and governments,

since they are a reversion to the old sanctification and sacralization of government policy, commonly use brain-washing, mental and physical torture, and liquidation against those who cannot conform to the official line. They cannot tolerate dissent, let alone opposition. And to make creative use of the loyal opposition, to learn by it and to live with it, is beyond their ken. The full, free, and informed discussion which is the oxygen of the open society is commonly derogated by totalitarians as "bourgeois" or "liberal" fallacy. If the spokesmen are thoroughly ideological, they may even explain that such "liberal" notions as freedom of speech, freedom of assembly and petition, freedom of the press, and freedom of religion belong to the nineteenth century—before "enlightened" men recognized the importance of economic determinism and ideological rectitude.

All this amounts to, in the end, is an ideological framework within which contemporary governments can act with the brutality of primitive regimes toward those who resist conformity.

In a rational and covenanted society, the fundamental and inalienable rights of free men are not given by government, but anteceded the frame of government. Government was created by the governed for specific ends, none higher than the enhancement of the liberties of citizens as persons and in their associations. The dream of a sacral monolith is retrogressive and reactionary, whether Communist or fascist. Marxism, contrary to much confusion among intellectuals, is reactionary and retrogressive.

[5] A NEW PERIODIZATION OF HISTORY. In ideological politics, the "elite" or "vanguard" carry history. In

most totalitarian thinkers there is a primitivist note: once there was a Golden Age, then came the Fall, and history will be completed with the seizure of power and the restitution of lost virtue. For Marx the "fall" was the advent of private property. In many American thinkers of fascist type the age of the "Founding Fathers" is mythologized as the Golden Age; whether the "fall" came with FDR or earlier is uncertain. In totalitarian thinking, the day of revolution, of the seizure of power, is the equivalent of the biblical Day of Judgment. Following this there is a period of transition, introduced by the slaying of the godless ("counter-revolutionaries," in modern language) and completed in "the withering away of the state." The final triumph of the millennial age of religious eschatology is secularized in a political description of the last and triumphant Age of Man.

Resentment toward the biblical author of history is evident in the effort to introduce new dating systems, as well as a new periodization of history: official papers are dated by "the Year 10 of the Fascist Revolution," the anniversary of the October Revolution assumes cultic significance, and the era of the party is to last 1,000 years. Nothing is resented more than "Anno Domini."

The pathos of areas conditioned to pathological parties and governments is everywhere apparent. It rings through the appeal of Christians in Communist East Germany: "Remember: we have lived for thirty-five years under totalitarian governments!" It shows in such special circumstances as called attention to by John Conway in his superb book, *The Nazi Persecution of the Churches, 1933–45*: documents held by the "German Democratic Republic" (*D.D.R*) are not readily available to western scholars.[3] From time to time the Communists loose political barrages against church-men or political leaders in the West, which may or may not be true, using documents which may or may not exist in the archives which they control. Whatever the circumstantial evidence, the presumption must always be negative when dealing with persons who reserve or limit to political use the primary sources. Of course the Communist purpose is the same as the Nazi: denying in principle the scholarly dialogue, they use or misuse or construct "sources" to fit ideological commitments.

The seriousness of the symbolic rewriting of the So-viet encyclopedia documents the point. In human life, the most tragic element is robbing youth of its heritage. The "now" generation is the beginning of a new *anthropos*, as we shall see; youth is turned away from the covenant of fathers and sons, away from the dia-logue with the "fallen" past, to dwell exclusively on history in the futuristic sense. The natural tension be-tween generations is exaggerated and exploited that the youth may become a fit tool of the revolution and the consummation of history. The Hungarian Revolt of 1956 in which young soldiers turned against their Communist rulers gave the lie to the myth; but it still persists among those who worship a mythical past and, in fact, despise history.

[6] A NEW ANTHROPOLOGY. The proletarianization of the mind of the youth (who are to be in the society but not of it before the revolution and the men of the future after it) is basic to the formation of "super-

[3] J. S. Conway, *The Nazi Persecution of the Churches, 1933–1945* (New York: Basic Books, Inc., 1968), p. xi; also p. xxix.

men." Both Nazi and Communist teaching declares
that the "new man" will be taller, healthier, possessing
greater brain capacity than man today. The young
toughs of the Hitler youth, of Mao's Red Guards, are
not just excessively loyal members of the party: they
are the young barbarians who, unhampered by consciousness of sin and guilt, build tomorrow's world. Like
the protagonist in Arthur Koestler's *The Age of Longing*, they are "natural," strong, without complexes and
without conscience or guilt.

The formation of the elite, which in the open society
is the work of the churches, is accomplished through
austere and rigorous political discipline. The mind is
brain-washed free of the illusions and values of the
"fallen" period. The secret discipline of the party makes
new men and new women, fit for the "modern" age.
("Modern" is a normative term for the totalitarian,
but not for the believing Jew or Christian.) The elite
acquire their own recognition symbols, their own special language.

If the new man ever tries to break out—and, to the
totalitarian, apostasy is far worse than nonmembership
—he becomes the "half-man" described by Whittaker
Chambers, Arthur Koestler, and the authors of *The
God That Failed*.

[7] THE ELITE. The "true believer" is fashioned into
a member of the group which carries history by the
secret discipline, and by the "secularized" cult of the
party. (The term "secularized," widely used by students of totalitarianism, is probably wrongheaded: totalitarianism is actually a remythologizing, a re-creation
of sacral society.) In both Communist and fascist parties there is a name-giving ceremony in substitution of

baptism; a *Jugendweihe* as alternative to confirmation or bar mitzvah; civic marriage ceremonies and civil committal services at the graveside displace the religious offices.

The concept of the "elite" or the "vanguard" is a corrupt adaptation of the biblical view of Israel as the carrier of history's meaning. The personality types which develop in totalitarian parties are imitative of the martyrs and confessors of true religion. The leadership types, the understanding of the party's function, the *Weltanschauung*—all can be understood only as "post-Christian" manifestations. Totalitarian *apparats* are, of course, perfectly capable of capturing and controlling primitive situations with no strong Christian background (*i.e.,* China, North Vietnam, Ghana). But without Christendom in decline, without the sour humors of the state churches of Russia and Germany and Italy and Spain, Stalin and Tito and Franco and Perón and Hitler would never have appeared. Without the decline of church discipline and the loss of integrity of church membership, those seeking sacrifice and devotion and service would never slide into Communist or fascist politico-religious structures of discipline.

The "psychology of the pawn," the psychology of the brain-washed who lives through all manner of personal degradation in the "critique" of the party cell, the studied contempt for personal integrity ("bourgeois morality") which marks both Communist and fascist movements—these are only intelligible as corruptions of religious practices and the self-hate of persons betraying their baptism.

[8] THE CULT OF VIOLENCE. In the redirection of ag-

gression, the praise of violence toward the opposition is fundamental. All totalitarian systems adulate the police and the military and delight in the use of brute force. The "devils" and the "godless" are to be wiped out: the totalitarian mind has no difficulty with capital punishment. There is a clear affinity of totalitarianism and militarism: military men, adulated, are preferred to simple civilians. "Support your local police!" is a favorite slogan of the John Birch Society, and letters to the editor express the wish that the police or storm troopers might be given a free hand with—for example —civil rights demonstrators. The former sheriff of Selma, Alabama, whose only claim to fame is that he used cattle prods on American citizens, is sponsored on lecture tours throughout the United States by the John Birch Society and its "fronts." Once power is seized, state power is used to liquidate dissenters.

The contempt for the Constitution and for law, which depends upon the controlled and limited use of violence, is frequently expressed in theoretical writings and agitational tracts. The "big lie" is used against faithful stewards of governmental office who resist totalitarian measures and movements: they are "Wall Street lackeys." The Dial-a-Lie telephone program of the John Birch Society, as well as the over 10,000 weekly radio programs of the agents of the radical right, are forms of sadism and barely subdued violence.

The agent mentality is cultivated, and renegades are preferred as witnesses: the atmosphere of personal vendettas carried by defrocked clergy and expelled party members is preferred to the steady and conscientious labors of those who have never succumbed to any form of totalitarianism. The work of such organizations as the CIA and FBI are, of course, necessary, but Congress has wisely provided that they shall be controlled by law and that their unsifted and un-evaluated materials shall not be broadcast recklessly in public. The amateur sleuths have no such hesitation, however, and both Communist and fascist organizations keep files on enemy persons and movements —using the data for character assassination now and liquidation later. In the American setting, the most unfortunate quasi-legal action has been the willingness of Congress to allow the House Internal Security Committee, formerly the House Un-American Activities Committee, to be used by fascist groups in violation of constitutional procedures and due process of law.

The amateur agents have created a new style of treason in our time, specialized in the "fifth column" which destroys constitutional order and trust, and developed large networks of espionage, subversion, and conspiracy. The so-called Church League of America boasts that its files contain the largest volume of negative information on individuals outside the FBI files. Their style of operation contrasts markedly with the neighborly work of loyal citizens, of persons who respect the Ninth Commandment, of those whose devotion to liberty has taught them respect for the persons and reputations of dissenters. They do not have the patience nor the staying power to practice self-government, and they are enthusiastic to destroy its restraints.

[9] THE INDUCEMENT OF SOCIAL APHASIA. Aphasia is that condition, either physical or psychological, which hampers or prevents a person from communicating with his fellows.

Pathological politics fattens on the breakdown of trust. At the same time that they profit by confusion, the extremists seek to promote further doubt and suspicion by constant attacks on the leaders of government, the churches and synagogues, the educational centers.

The final end of the breakdown of trust is the bureaucratic police state, where every decision must be checked and counterchecked by a host of paranoid inspectors. The most vivid recent description is found in Alexander Solzhenitsyn's novel about life in the Soviet Union: *The Cancer Ward* (Bantam Books, 1969). Even the requisitoning of cleaning rags for the wards has become a matter of suspicion, requiring signatures and countersignatures by three top officials of the hospital.

Christians have always known that the burdens of power and decision are great, and that those to whom we have in God's name entrusted the ordinance of government need the prayers of the church that they be faithful stewards. Nothing is further from the church's attitude to those in authority than the constant slander and scorn which is the style of pathological political groups and parties.

Ideological politics produces a breed of demagogues, of individuals taught to take a bad case and win at all costs. The compulsive and irrational utterances of totalitarian spokesmen could be heard during the Third Reich over the Berlin *Sender,* can be heard now over Mao's Peking radio, and provide the regular diet of the night radio in America as the radical right pollutes the air waves daily. The manipulation of mobs is their specialty.

The purpose of the totalitarian is to break down the full, free, and informed discussion which is the oxygen of the life of liberty. Having distinguished between "education" (of the inner ranks) and the "propaganda" (directed to those outside the fold), the totalitarian leaders broadcast from a soundproof room to the society at large. They are opposed to life in the Age of Dialogue: "government by discussion" is a "liberal fallacy." Proletarianized in mind and spirit—*i.e.*, in the society but not of it—they deny the obligation to communicate with fellow citizens in matters concerning the public good. Anonymous opinions are peddled, by voice or in writing, to destroy the reputations and standing of those who sign their names to their positions. The "open face of truth" commended in the New Testament is denied and scorned. In the training of demagogues and in the destruction of unintimidated discussion in the public forum, as nowhere else so openly, the totalitarians show themselves for what they are: well poisoners and grave diggers. Especially noteworthy is the attack on the colleges and universities, and the propensity to found fly-by-night "colleges" of no academic status. For the charter of the academy, both classical and modern, is the promotion of a raging dialogue; therefore, both Communists and fascists make sport of the professors and demand that the students be kept "under control."

The inducement of social aphasia, that is, the breakdown of open access and open-faced communication, is pressed on by totalitarian movements through terrorization of other movements and by skillful use of the "gatekeeper" position within the party. When power has been seized, the "gatekeeper"—to whom go all reports and from whom all orders issue forth—destroys the last remnants of neighborly discussion. The spread of the town meeting is, therefore, a specific against *Gleichschaltung*. When Hitler died in the bunker, completely out of touch with reality—ordering into battle armies that no longer existed, and calling up air armadas that had never been built—he played the latter end of the enemy of free and responsible communication. God is not mocked!

One of the reasons why totalitarianism is a modern development, different in kind from ancient tyrannies and despotisms, is that only with radio and telephone and television have the instruments of communication been so concentrated in control that a relatively small number of "true believers" can control the communications system of millions of people. There is no longer the distance, there are no longer the autonomous communities, there is no longer the time lag which protected earlier generations from the all-penetrating and cancerous effect of totalitarian ideas and controls. This is one reason why the fight of the Institute for American Democracy against air pollution by the radical right is a battle for nothing less than the mind and soul of America.

[10] THE POLICE STATE.   The totalitarian is an advocate of police and military autonomy independent of civilian control. In a system of liberty and self-government, the use of violence is carefully controlled, and those who are agents of the laws are kept on the leash. In the totalitarian system, murder and arson and torture and terror are standard weapons of the politically tainted police. The totalitarian age is the age of lawless policemen, disloyal generals, and adulation of those assigned to administer violence. The self-styled "liberals" who delight to relate the Communist destruction of the *kulaks* and the bourgeois in Russia and

China are of the same mind-set as the self-styled "conservatives" who want to loose the police or the stormtroopers upon protesting citizens. The concentration camp, whether in Vorkuta or Dachau or Angola or China, is the symbol of the totalitarian system.

Against the demonic police state, those who love liberty and self-government hold the police and the army subject to civilian review. They stand for a government of law, not of men. They declare and practice respect for the liberty and integrity of persons, including the stranger in the land (*e.g.*, the Amish). In place of organized posses and direct action, they defend constitutional guarantees and due process of law.

The totalitarian age differs from the old tyrannies in this: the technological concentration of power in the hands of a very few makes possible a defiance of the will of the general citizenry which could not exist earlier. Today, two tank divisions can suppress a revolution supported by 16½ million people (June 17, 1953, in East Germany) four tank divisions suffice to put down a popular revolt equipped with small arms (October 26 to November 7, 1956, in Hungary). The crisis in Jeffersonian thought is acute: revolution by "the people" is no longer possible in industrial societies, and, once the totalitarians are lodged in power, they cannot be removed without outside help.

[11] MONOLITHIC PARTY AND/OR STATE. The design of the totalitarian party or state is the wheel, with hubs and spokes. At the hub is the party leadership, the leader, and all sections of the society are directly controlled by those to whom all other human centers are but "fronts" for ideological purposes. Independent centers of thought and initiative are suppressed; even

the pro-Hitler fraternities were suppressed by the Nazis,
lest independent action might accidentally develop in
their midst. Since the party is an instrument of salvation and the leader is a savior figure, nothing else in
the created order is entitled to integrity or respect.
Demagoguery and ecstatic utterances swing the masses;
strict discipline controls the initiated. All divided sovereignty, whether federal or pluralistic, is resented and
systematically undermined.

Especially important to the lover of liberty is the
existence of strong centers of thought and discipline
separate from the state. In business and industry, both
the private *and* the public sectors are important. In
higher education, a two-track system of state *and* independent colleges is vital. Important too are those civic
groups which express spontaneous initiatives and chan-
nel civic concern along a different track or even in conflict with the hierarchical, power-aligned, tribal "fellowship" *(Gemeinschaft)*. To the advocate of responsible self-government, the application of pietistic notions of self-absorption in the social body to the political arena is a clear perversion of the religious motif.

[12] THE BEAUTIFUL STATE.   The totalitarian, lacking a
genuine doctrine of sin, regards the ambiguities and im-
perfections of life in history as something which can
be sloughed off with a change of conditions. Lord
Bryce once pointed out that the genius of the American Constitution, with its checks and balances, derives
from the Founding Fathers' awareness of the reality
of original sin. The totalitarian mind, unable to come
to terms with life, blames "the politicians" or some
"conspiracy" for situations which are actually intelligible only in terms of the human tragedy itself. The

Docetic mind-set, which cannot tolerate "compromise" and other earthiness, gives religious support to the purity and sincerity and simplicity of totalitarian solutions. As Walter Bagehot pointed out, an awareness of "the doubtfulness things are involved in" is a mark of maturity; but totalitarian groups are, by mood, the politics of adolescence, and there is no room for doubt or ambiguity among them. An awareness of guilt and doubt is a mark of sin against the party and not to be tolerated in Messianic politics. For a subject to doubt the party's program and leadership is the only "sin."

[13] FALSE CONSENSUS. The building up and sustaining of the public opinion is a general responsibility among free men, and it requires self-discipline of a high order. The totalitarian groups, however, ignore the dialogue and practice the politics of the end-time. Acceptance of the intention to live with the opposition, willingness to compromise and to stick to the prudential rather than quest the ultimate, come hard to Communists and fascists. The pseudo-democracy of the Communist "peoples' democracies," like the pseudo-conservatism of the radical right, uses the language of self-government without the content. The general will, interpreted at a given moment without regard to the covenant of fathers and sons, is put forward to excuse mob rule and its supremacy over constitutional due process. A false consensus is declared by demagogues or false leaders: a true consensus can only emerge after the fullest and most thorough discussion of the alternatives, a discussion in which all who share in the consequences of the decision have a part.

[14] RELIANCE UPON THE ORAL TRADITION of the tribal group, of the natural society. The most common practical evidence of this is the contempt for written documents, for carefully sifted evidence, for critically appraised facts. Adventurers and defrocked preachers are preferred over honest citizens. The cult of the renegades is cultivated: in the radical right in America, the opinions of individuals who lied as Communists and now lie as fascists is preferred over the documented evidence of persons with names and faces and honest credentials.

The desire of totalitarians to return to the tribal "fellowship" has been mentioned above. Tied to this is the preference for "what everyone knows"—*i.e.*, rumor, gossip, scandal, and slander—over original sources critically assessed. The Soviet historians must regularly rewrite the Soviet Encyclopedia; the anti-Semites peddle the forged Protocols of the Elders of Zion; the radical right circulates false (and usually anonymous) reports on the National Council of Churches, the leaders of government, and the leaders of the churches. Where the old and forgotten language of the ethnic group cannot be reclaimed, a new esoteric language is developed. With ecstatic songs and phrases and a cultivation of the group mind, the critical and sceptical mind of the civilized man is numbed and brain-washed and enslaved.

[15] DETERMINISM. The "fates," whether interpreted as economic determinism or a new parallel to the decline and fall of Rome, take precedence over the citizen's personal responsibility and obligation to choose. The religious doctrine of providence is made political. The seizure of power by the elite or vanguard is not

just desirable; it is inevitable. The kind of certainty about the last things which marks high religion becomes the style of ideological politics.

By this process the agony of real choice is lifted from the individual. His secret consciousness of sin, in his bad faith toward neighbors and fellow citizens, is purged. The world and its institutions are filled with persons who, like the assassin Oswald, yearn to play a central part in "the verdict of history." By this means both sharing in social guilt and atonement for personal guilt are rendered useless, indeed "counter-revolutionary."

Not all of the totalitarian groups are Communist or fascist, although on the world map and internally these are the most serious threats. The Mafia, for instance, fits the "grid" on a number of points. Even more obvious, so does Sokagakkai—a paramilitary and political party in Japanese Buddhism which is gaining adherents among American military personnel.

Distinctions must be made, with the refinement of the typology and the clarification of the "grid." For instance, fascist groups tend to regress toward tribal loyalties, whereas Communist movements are a false cosmism. Even here, however, the "grid" is more accurate than popular belief would have it: under pressure in World War II, Russian communism went pan-Slav and ethnic, and the pride of the Chinese race is an important support of Mao; both fascism and Nazism had their universal claims. There is today a fascist international, as the cooperation of leaders of America's spiritual underworld (such as Hargis, Bundy, and McIntire) with the governments of South Africa and Rhodesia indicate. Right now the fascist international is a rather pitiful affair contrasted with the mortal threat posed by the Communist international, but the "grid" does not require as much adjustment at this point as some suppose.

The final point is that further study will be needed for some time to take the initiative away from the racketeers and relieve the pressure upon professional government agencies, which are forbidden by law to answer back. At Iowa Wesleyan College, basic plans have recently been laid for a Center of Social Pathology, the first of its kind in the country. If the "grid" is as revealing as I think, and if the challenge of totalitarianism is as important for all phases of the intellectual enterprise as here claimed, in the years to come there will be such a Center of Social Pathology in every serious institute of study. Precisely in this way, new disciplines enter the republic of learning as fields of interdisciplinary and voluntary cooperation and become in time departments and schools of their own. More important yet, as students learn creative and responsible citizenship on campus, their parents can, in study groups centering down on social pathology, come to understand both the nature of sick societies and the style of those still relatively healthy.

III

---·--·--·---

Totalitarianism: "Grid II" (Practical)

··

THE study of social pathology has both theoretical and practical import. In college and university the definition of totalitarian systems and movements affords an unusual opportunity for interdisciplinary study and for advancing political theory. The development of a dependable typology is a useful academic exercise. It also has great importance for the enactment and administration of laws suitable to the defense of constitutional liberty and self-government. Grid I is intended for theological use and for political theoretical work: it is intended to clarify principles which distinguish the totalitarian world view from the pragmatic style of politics. For use in everyday life, at the level where political decisions are made and carried through, Grid II is elaborated. There is considerable overlay between the two—Grid I concerned with theory and Grid II

93

with action—because the strike for power is implicit
in every totalitarian ideology. Both the Communists
and the John Birch Society have repeatedly attempted
to portray themselves as associations devoted to "political education": in fact, however—as in the extraor-
dinary effort of the Birchers on behalf of George Wallace's candidacy—the totalitarians have an unfailing
instinct for the jugular. They are fascinated by the use
of power; they are disciplined to capture it.

The ordinary citizen, who cares little for conflicting
world views but much for what he calls "fair play,"
may recognize the totalitarian action or system or party
quite as quickly as the learned scholar. In fact, the gap
between thought and action which is the disease of the
academics may be much less advanced in his case, and
his largely intuitive responses to action which are outside the bounds of common decency may be more direct and more useful in a given situation than the
tendency of professors to watch and describe crucifix-
ions "objectively." To the extent that the citizen's
political instincts have been formed by our American
constitutional heritage, he will know the difference
between loyal opposition and internal defection—even
though he might be hard put to it to define either in a
literarily acceptable way.

The totalitarian, whether Communist or fascist,
repudiates truths and values and commitments which
are disengaged from immediate action. Ideology, the
systematic elaboration of ideas which are tools of
political action, is an intimate part of every totalitarian
party's arsenal. Grid II, however, is intended to help
define and make recognizable the totalitarian style of
political action to persons not accustomed to think
theoretically and not devoted to a world view which

makes the distinction between Grid I and Grid II impossible.

The chief marks of totalitarian action and politics follow.

1. Anti-Semitic propaganda is frequently present among Communists and black extremists as well as among fascists. Sometimes, especially among gentlemanly anti-Semites, it is disguised as "anti-Zionist" propaganda; this escapes momentarily the scandal of vulgar anti-Semitism, but the political consequences are the same. It is a distinction without a difference, whether purveyed by the neo-Nazis of Germany (who are today all "anti-Zionist" but never openly anti-Semitic), the propaganda agents of the Arab League (who are carefully "anti-Zionist" in the United States but say what they mean at home), or by various cultured "liberal" churchmen who are embarrassed by vulgar anti-Semitism but teach a Marcionite Christianity which manages to be anti-Jewish at each specific political decision.

Those Christian groups which cooperate with Jews, such as the National Conference of Christians and Jews, as well as the major Jewish agencies (B'nai B'rith Anti-Defamation League, the American Jewish Committee, and the United Jewish Appeal), are constantly attacked.

At the level of direct action, totalitarian groups engage in the bombing of synagogues, defacement of Jewish buildings and cemeteries, slander of Jewish community leaders and public officials, discrimination against Jewish merchants or firms or educators, boycotts of companies trading with Israel, exclusion of Jews from membership in voluntary associations, and campaigns against candidates for public office who are Jews or presumed to be such.

Perhaps the most scandalous illustration of fascist exploitation of anti-Semitism in American politics during 1968 was the attack led by Senator James Eastland on the nomination of Justice Abe Fortas to be Chief Justice of the United States Supreme Court. Eastland was guilty of violating basic canons of decency in his management of the Judiciary Committee hearings, and he organized a field day for "testimony" by all of the major fascist and anti-Semitic organizations opposing the Fortas nomination. In the end, the nomination was withdrawn to save further embarrassment for a lame duck president—the first time in American history that the Senate violated constitutional propriety in giving consent to a proper exercise of presidential powers of appointment.

Earl Raab, executive director of the Jewish Community Relations Council of San Francisco, has recently pointed out publicly one of the most dangerous developments among some black militants. This is the extent to which some of the younger spokesmen have been deliberately using anti-Semitic slogans to attract the support of the unreasoning and prejudiced. The dangerous possibility is that white politicians, unwilling to cut the blacks in on their political and economic power structure, will encourage a diversionary anti-Semitism—much as reactionary governments in eastern Europe have long diverted the peasants from real issues by using the Jew as a scapegoat.

The status of black militancy is highly volatile since the death of Dr. Martin Luther King, Jr. As long as Dr. King remained the chief spokesman for the hopes and programs of black citizens, Christianity provided the ruling guidelines, and the Gandhian philosophy and method of nonviolent direct action effected change combined with reconciliation. With dozens vying to be his successor—most of them without confidence in Christianity and lacking any disciplined ideology—anti-Semitic appeals are becoming more common. Rap Brown and Stokely Carmichael have both been guilty of such demagoguery. John Hatcher, for a short time head of the Martin Luther King, Jr., Center at New York University, was guilty of vulgar anti-Semitism in public addresses. During the Populist period, politicians in power succeeded in turning the poor whites against the Negroes and preventing the formation of a popular movement which could have forced economic readjustment. It would be tragic indeed if today the black leadership were to allow itself to be similarly diverted from the main issue by another diversionary trick.

Most important in the long run, however, is the possibility that the recovery of black pride and self-identity might fall into the same regressive pattern as that of other gentile tribalisms. Theologically, black anti-Semitism represents the same potential retreat from history as Teutonic or Anglo-Saxon ethnicity. Significantly, the rise of black anti-Semitism parallels the emergence of black ideology and totalitarian organization. For at least a century, and perhaps before that, the black Christians in America afforded the most true appropriation of biblical identity and the most authentic representation of Christian faithfulness. As young blacks turn away from Christianity, as their ablest spokesmen ignore the seminaries and turn to new schools of ideology, there is a real possibility that the black leaders of the years immediately ahead may be as low-grade as Lester Maddox, James Eastland, Strom Thurmond, and

Leander Perez among the whites. Racist ideology is a two-edged sword, and, whether white or black, it represents a betrayal of high religion and also of the American dream. If a definite trend occurs in that direction, active anti-Semitism will be evident for some time before open attacks on the churches become frequent.

Anti-Semitism became an overt force in the United States during the last quarter of the nineteenth century, where the rising competition of a new Jewish middle class threatened the dominant middle class of older settlers. Early Puritanism, strong in both New England's standing order and the Church of England of the middle and southern colonies, was characteristically long in use of the Old Testament and strong in friendship toward the Jews. In the twentieth century, the founding of anti-Semitic organizations has clearly paralleled (1) the decline of Calvinist theology in American Protestantism, and (2) the rise of political anti-Semitism as an ideological weapon of political fascism. An important study "records the founding of five anti-Semitic organizations in the United States between 1915 and 1922, nine in 1933, and 105 between 1934-39—a clear indication of the rapid increase in organized prejudice during the 1930's." [1] Many of those individuals presently leading anti-Semitic organizations in the radical right were under surveillance during World War II for their pro-Nazi activities, and some were even brought to court. Both their politics and their "religion" have been disloyal to American legal tradition and the standards of the American Protestant churches before they declined into the status of social establishments (culture-religions).

[1] G. Simpson and M. Yinger, *Racial and Cultural Minorities* (New York: Harper & Bros., 1953), p. 290.

The development of totalitarian regimes in areas outside the "Christian world" would seem to challenge the thesis that totalitarianism is essentially "post-Christian" and that anti-Semitism is endemic to it. Japan was undoubtedly a totalitarian state during World War II. Mainland China is governed by a totalitarian structure today. The relationship of modern technology to militarism and to governments which operate on a war basis, even though "non-Christian," deserves special attention. Nevertheless, there is ample evidence of the effect of Christian views of history upon "non-Christian" peoples and nations, as shown in the emergence of Hindu and Muslim and Buddhist renewal movements plainly influenced by the Christianity they reject. Moreover, specialized studies of totalitarian ideologies arising in "non-Christian" civilizations—such as a recent brilliant treatment of *The Taiping Ideology*—quite clearly demonstrate the influence of Christian theological and historical views.

In any case, there can be no argument about the role of anti-Semitism in all totalitarian movements in "Christendom." the *apartheid* majority in the present parliament of South Africa is viciously anti-Semitic, and many of its leaders were openly pro-Hitler during World War II. During the Russian rape of Czechoslovakia, the re-establishment of Russian hegemony was accompanied by purges of Jewish intellectuals and politicians.[2] During the nineteenth century, Tsarist

[2] On the Czech purges, see *The New York Times* reports: i.e., Sept. 3, 1968, covering *Izvestia's* attack on Hajek, Kriegel, Sik, Goldstuecker. As with anti-Semites of the less vulgar type in the United States, the present Communist attack on the Jews professes to be "anti-Zionist" and "pro-Arab" rather than openly anti-Semitic, the latter posture being embarrassing to many intellectuals since the period of the Third Reich in Germany.

Russia was the most savagely anti-Semitic government in the world, and the Communist rulers of Russia have used the same tool from time to time to arouse primitive emotions and divert attention from policy or program failures. The story in Poland is the same, and within recent months the remaining Polish Jews have been subjected again to rescript and quota in education and politics.

2. Since totalitarian politics breeds demagoguery, sophistry rather than dialogue, ambiguous ideological slogans are common: "A choice, not an echo," "Let's get in or get out," "America is a republic, not a democracy," "Register communists, not guns," "Support your local police," and other substitutes for thinking.

"Support your local police!" is another typical bit of demagoguery. Every taxpayer supports his local police. The question is whether the police shall be supported when they violate the Constitution, when they become wolves instead of defenders of the sheep, when they become the center of illegality. Shall we "support our police" when they murder three students in Orangeburg, South Carolina? Shall we "support our police" when they murder three students registering voters in Philadelphia, Mississippi? Shall we "support our police" when they murder two young black men in a Detroit motel? The John Birchers and other fascists would have us do so, just as their spiritual brothers support their police in beating up the intellectuals in Mao's China, just as their "soul brothers" supported the police in murdering dissenters and Jews in the Third Reich.

The loyal American, however, will remember that the police—like other vocational and professional groups—have a stewardship. The stewardship of the police is, as the old Christian prayer phrased it, to "protect the innocent, restrain the wicked, and to keep their hands from innocent blood." When the lawless policeman begins to show his face, the loyal American will insist that he be restrained by the law of God and the law of the land—just like the abortionist doctor, the crooked lawyer, and the gangster-serving politician. So far, most policemen are still loyal Americans— although the number displaying Wallace buttons in the 1968 election was dismaying. Loyal policemen are entitled to the prayers of the Christians, the assistance of the citizens, and the support of the government. Lawless policemen, of the kind both Communists and fascists admire and cultivate, belong in prison.

Slogans of this type are a substitute for thinking, and they are intended to function as such. "A choice, not an echo," was a popular slogan of the radical right during the 1964 presidential campaign, and it was so successful in polarizing opinion that the extremists captured the Republican nomination in San Francisco. Robert Welch, dictator of the John Birch Society, was able to boast that over a hundred of the voting delegates to the Republican Convention were members of the society. Candidate Goldwater's chief political adviser, Stephen Shadegg, boasted after Goldwater's defeat, "Now we're down to the hard core!" This is authentic Trotskyite thinking, and, in fact, Shadegg admitted in print his indebtedness to Chairman Mao of China for lessons in political tactics. To the credit of the Republican party regulars at the 1968 Miami Convention, the extremists were there held in check: the sensible people, moderates, decided they "didn't want to go over Niagara Falls again." The extremist wing viewed the most appalling defeat ever suffered by an American presidential candidate as an exercise in political tactics, however, and many split off to work for a Wallace victory. Wallace's planned "victory" was not, of course, a clean mandate: it was to create enough third-party strength to be able to manipulate and deal behind the scenes.

Whether America is a "republic" or a "democracy," and here the Hamiltonian and Jeffersonian traditions— both authentically American—tend to divide, the one thing certain is that neither a republic nor a democracy can survive if any large number of voters goes over to Communist or fascist polarization tactics. The play on words advanced by the extremists is intended to divert attention from their basic disloyalty to the Constitution, the public dialogue, and moderation of either a "liberal" or "conservative" type. Their goal is power, and they are prepared to pull down the pillars of the American temple of politics to realize their ambition. The goal of responsible people is to strengthen the middle ground, to extend the dialogue to include all persons entitled to help decide their present and future, and rigorously to exclude those who intend not dialogue but the rule of the knife.

Demagoguery is just as common in leftist extremism as in rightist circles. Among the most blatant illustrations are the use made of the Rosenberg case in France and other foreign countries and the sloganizing protests against American policy in Southeast Asia in many European areas. At home the most serious development is the rise of Maoist influence among Students for a Democratic Society. The literature of the "new left" is increasingly characterized, in the last year and a half, by demagogic slogans which substitute for specific suggestions, rational programs, reasonable change.

3. The use of polarizing slurs against opponents ("hunkie," "comsymps," or "bourgeois") is intended not only to destroy the middle and moderate ground but to shame compromise solutions. Pedestrian politics has sometimes been called "the science of compromise," and against compromise of any kind the totalitarian mentality—which defines all issues in black and white—has permanent opposition.

In civilized debate terms of courtesy are used in reference to the opponent as well as the ally. Immature discussants, like primitive peoples universally, "take everything personally": the difficult art of public dialogue distinguishes between the person of the opponent and his views. The mature discussant is aware of the doubtfulness of every real decision, and he knows that the debate must continue another day on another decision. Helmut Gollwitzer, one of the German churchmen most active in opposition to the Nazis and now the Communists, has said that the genius of the English/American political system is precisely the intention of participants to live with the opposition: ideological politics intends only to wipe them out.

For this reason totalitarian politics has been called "the politics of adolescence." Parades replace discussion, symbols (including slogans) replace reasoned discourse, street fighting and the rule of the knife mark the regression to the primitive short-cuts to consensus. Self-government is a recent and difficult development in the affairs of mankind, and those who have not grown up to it are constantly tempted to regress into the kind of mob action which defies reason and denies the integrity and dignity of the opposition.

4. To the totalitarian, politics becomes the ultimate science, and political decisions have to do with ultimates. To the man of liberty, politics has to do with pragmatic decisions and the "god-talk" is limited to the religious covenant. The slogans which reveal the eschatological nature of totalitarian politics are many: "German faith," "German greeting," (*Heil Hitler!*), "Christian America," "peoples' democracies," "racial purity," "the will of the Founding Fathers," etc. The answer of the man of conscience is to insist that ultimate commitments belong only in the religous covenant, and political decisions are limited to the human measure.

In all primitive societies, and in most of the history of mankind up to the rise of self-government and liberty, political commitment and religious obligation were one and the same. "Heresy" and "treason" were interchangeable terms, since disobedience to a ruler by divine right was both a political and religious offense. Among the most advanced societies, where the religious and the political covenants have been separated, a man may be a good citizen even though he belongs to an unpopular religious group, and he may be a faithful man of religion even though he dissent from some action of the government.

5. Totalitarian ideologies involve the resacralization of society and politics, to the destruction of conscience and the abasement of liberty. A new periodization is introduced into historical discussion, signalized by such slogans as "the Year 10 of the Fascist Revolution,"

"The Thousand Years' Reich," "the Day of Reckoning," and "the Final Conflict."

To the Jew and Christian, history is defined [and periodized] along biblical lines. The Christian lives in "*Anno Domini.*" The pseudo-religious nature of the totalitarian myths shows up in the effort to redefine history, its direction, and its consummation. The man who lives within the atmosphere and thought world of the Bible knows that all political events are temporal and transitory, that no possible political action will change the basic nature of sinful man, that the creation of "new men" and "new women" is a work of the Holy Spirit and not of the party.

In the American setting, no myth is more overworked by the totalitarians than that of the "Founding Fathers." The Founding Fathers, however, knew themselves to be mortal and also were wise to construct a limited ("creaturely") frame of government—leaving to the churches the matters of the end-time.

6. The totalitarian effort is directed to splitting this generation of youth from its elders, turning the young against their heritage and against all tradition. "The modern generation," "the now generation," hostility to "the Establishment," hostility toward persons "over thirty"—such are not accidental slogans or attitudes, but the carefully cultivated work of both Communist and fascist movements.

In the healthy society the relationship between the generations is one of creative tension. The natural impatience of youth is balanced by the tolerance which grows with maturity: the youth are impatient with the wrongs and the injustices but loving and charitable toward their elders—who also suffered, were defeated in some hopes and triumphant in others. In the sick society the youth has turned against the previous generations and pridefully thinks of itself as a new generation freed from mortality and error. My late friend, Bishop Otto Dibelius of the Church of Berlin-Brandenburg—himself an opponent of the Nazis and the Communists—once told me that the basic issue between the Christians and the totalitarians was "anthropology." He meant that to the totalitarians human nature is shaped by the party and redeemed by the revolution, whereas to the Christian human nature is only changed in Christ.

One of the most striking of contemporary sculptures is by Knud C. Knudsen, a young German artist who himself managed to survive years of opposition to the Nazis. The set is called "The Generations," and a copy is found in the entrance to Bad Boll Evangelical Academy near Stuttgart. "The Generations" shows Moses and Joshua, portrayed on Mount Pisgah in that moment when the old man is informed by God that he will not go down into the promised land, but that a young man shall lead the people. Joshua is portrayed in fine and moving lines, impatient, unscarred by life, eager to move forward. Moses is portrayed in benedictory stance, lined by the years, stretching out the hand of blessing. The two figures are separate, yet they are joined at the base; and at the base stand too the tablets of the law. The younger generation and the older are linked by a basic commitment, by the covenant of fathers and sons; the tradition is passed, to be transmitted and transmuted. Their outstretched hands do not touch, but rather stretch toward each other in the motion of runners passing the baton. This is the "covenant of fathers and sons" of the Bible, the "communion of saints" of the creed. This is the right relationship between the generations.

Christians and Jews can never embrace an apocalyptic creed which splits the generations, which turns the young against their elders, which professes to produce a new generation such as never has existed on earth before. Persons informed by the Bible can never accept the anthropology of the totalitarians, who turn the human tragedy into a political comedy.

7. In totalitarian life, the party substitutes for the church, and the leaders of the party take the place of the saints. The cultic practices of the party replace the happenings of high religion. A party liturgy emerges: name-giving in the party replaces baptism, marriages in the party replace the religious service and covenant, party marriages—often performed en masse—replace religious vows, party puberty rites (*Jugendweihe!*) become a substitute for Christian confirmation or bar mitzvah, pilgrimages to party shrines—often primitive and superstitious—take the place of religious holy places. The thousands who line up at Lenin's tomb are, objectively speaking, engaged in the same sort of service as the thousands who line up at Lourdes or Fatima.

The totalitarians have developed party shrines of awesome significance: Lenin's tomb, the Franco Valley of Heroes, the spot where Hort Wessel was "martyred" in Munich. Political saints emerge: John Reed, John Birch, Horst Wessel, the Rosenbergs. A secret discipline is developed among the initiates, replacing the *disciplina arcana* of the primitive Christians. Secret and mysterious signals develop—both optical and verbal—which serve in general meetings to identify the initiates to each other. The totalitarians enter general meetings, especially in organizations which they plan to take over, with hidden agenda.

In the totalitarian view, history is carried by the "elite" or the "vanguard"—professional, disciplined revolutionaries. Careful distinction is made between "members" and "followers": the former are "educated," the latter are objects of propaganda. The view of the select people carrying history is a vulgarization of the biblical doctrine of the elect and is another evidence of the corruption of religious truth to fit party interests.

8. Symbols of sadism and violence are approved, with praise for the police actions which intimidate and terrify dissenters. Civilian control of the military and of the police is opposed; civilian review boards are bitterly fought. The liquidation of "counter-revolutionaries"—as in Russia, Spain, Germany, Communist China, Greece—it a clear political policy. Disloyal generals are praised and featured in public meetings. Cross burnings and lynchings are used. Movie films and anonymous telephone and radio programs attack the persons and characters of public leaders who have refused to go along. Defrocked preachers and renegade Communists are preferred to honest witnesses with a record of probity. The more vulgar and vicious forms of sedition are encouraged by disloyal public officials, with unpunished arson and murder the results.

9. The totalitarian reversion to primitive "justice" is shown in the regression to mob demonstrations, mob violence, and the "trial" of public figures in mob assembly. Town meetings, the classical expression of

popular democracy, are either taken over or attacked as subversive. Groups sponsoring full, free, and informed discussion are attacked: colleges and universities, the League of Women Voters, churches, and trade unions. Extremist radio and television programs—e.g., Paul Harvey—are featured and financed in place of panels and open discussion. "Fronts" are set up to deceive the "innocents"; this is a favorite tactic of both Communists and John Birchers (TACT, American Forum, Train, etc.). By a holding company operation, the control group is able to create an impression of widespread public support which does not in fact represent any independent initiative or discussion.

10. The attack on constitutional government and the Bill of Rights (First Amendment, Fifth Amendment, Fourteenth Amendment) is pressed with massive assault on the President, Supreme Court, members of Congress who refuse to go along, the two-party system. Strangers in the land, like the Old Mennonites and Hutterites and Jehovah's Witnesses, are persecuted. Ad hoc committees and posses replace channels and structures of due process. Tribal assembly and direct action are preferred to weighty and reasoned decision. Finally, police state emergency measures become permanent methods for dealing with issues.

11. Totalitarians, with their polarizing mentality, lay claim to exclusive possession of the truth, bolstered by "inside-dopester" assertions of a paranoid type: that the national government is run by Communists and socialists; that the American commitment in Southeast Asia is a result of secret control of public policy by an "industrial-military complex"; that the governments in

Washington and Moscow are but two arms of one body ("the Insiders"). Party cells and caucuses are organized to take over PTA's, school boards, posts in state legislatures and the federal Congress, trade unions, and professional associations. In the areas of parliamentary government, the totalitarians aim first at the post of ministry of the interior; in voluntary organizations, the target is the executive secretary post; in state governments, it is the post of attorney general which is most sought. The totalitarian instinct for power is expressed in the drive for key control posts, which, when captured, are used freely and often illegally against persons and groups of other views.

12. Excessive claims are made for what can be accomplished once power is "in the right hands." The assault on the present structures of authority in colleges and universities is usually based on some real grievance, but the aim is a total revolution—not the resolution of any specific problem. The uses of government, of the "state," are glorified—even if both Communists and fascists claim their ultimate goal is the withering away of the state. The drive for positions of power and for control of government gives the lie to the claims to emphasize human values and independence of the individual.

13. Political "critique" and group confession are used among members to enforce conformity and coerce deviation. Political exorcism is a standard practice of totalitarians of all kinds, and internal trials are held as a substitute for open, due process of law. The worst sin is to depart from party discipline once having joined the initiates, far worse than never to have joined.

"Consensus" is forced, not genuine. The disciplined and proletarianized movement becomes a weapon for action in the public arena.

14. The myth of the past is expressed in present action, looking to a future which will restore tribal or ethnic virtue long lost. Ethnic identity is romanticized ("Teutonic virtue," "Anglo-Saxon genius," "black identity," and "Christian America"). Racial discrimination points toward eventual apartheid. Racial homogeneity is pursued, and culture is interpreted in racist terms. Contempt for written documents, individual achievements, and objective evidence is shown in the reversion to dependence upon tribal memory (rumors, superstitions, primitive symbols). The critical and comparative method is ridiculed (*i.e.*, the attack on the RSV). Ecstatic utterance and unrestrained partisanship are cultivated among leaders and initiates; the ability to see both sides of a question is scorned as a residuum of "bourgeois mentality," or "liberal illusion."

15. A dogmatic style of political utterance reveals the essentially religious conviction that the very stars in their courses fight on the side of the party. The closed mind, hostility to open dialogue and fair play to opponents, subversion of due process in the conduct of organizations and public meetings—all indicate a self-righteousness about the fates which is deterministic. The individual conscience is relieved of guilt, and the party is thereby able to win fellow travelers among the weak and uncertain.

16. The critical question is this: Who has a right to participate in the dialogue? Persons who value liberty, and who have often joined battle to defend the

basic freedoms against primitive forms of suppression, have had great difficulty in meeting the extremist threat at an effective level. The Communist party and the John Birch Society both portray themselves as "opinion" groups, and the decent person—who has learned to honor and defend the liberty of other persons, even when he abhors their views—finds it hard to bring himself to act effectively to reduce the influence of those whose aim is power, and whose victory means death to human liberty. The result is that well-meaning people often spend more time providing a forum for totalitarians than for those of reasonable views, and in listening to the extremists than to those who have something to contribute to the public opinion.

Yet a critical distinction is possible and must be made, if in the end the costs are not to be far higher. The distinction is this: the totalitarians are not politically abhorrent because of their wild ideas and wild tongues, but because of their style and their lust for power. The Communist party and the John Birch Society, the Progressive Labor party and RAM are not organs of opinion-forming and discussion at all: they are instruments of subversion, machines of ideological warfare. Those who defy the rules of the dialogue, who use the knife against those who disagree with them, have no moral right to participate in the dialogue. The rule of thumb is this: I do not intend to listen to persons who will not listen to me. Although the pastor or the family member may have a special case in relation to someone under totalitarian discipline, in the society as a whole it must be recognized that he does not intend discussion but power, not fair play and mutual edification but war to the hilt.

We may despise the racist opinions of the Ku Klux

Klan, but the legal distinction between advocacy and action protects the members from suppression for opinions alone. We may despise the self-righteous pseudo-patriotism of the Minutemen, one of the most dangerous of American fascist movements, but their right to express unsavory views is protected by the Constitution. There is, however, no protected right to mobilize a conspiracy, raise money for it, publish recruitment literature, train revolutionaries. These are objectively determinable facts which make action against them justifiable and proper.

The crisis of totalitarianism is a crisis of law, not of opinion. Organizations which qualify under ten to twelve points of either "grid" should be suppressed, and persons who participate in their conspiracies and subversive activities should be penalized at law. Again, we are not advocating the organization of posses—although war is a giant posse action, and it has frequently been made inevitable in this century because structures of law and due process were not developed in time to deal nonviolently with those who strike at the vitals of civilized life.

So far, no real effort has been made to create a body of law to deal with totalitarian conspiracies—with the exception of a short-lived but very successful policy in the German Federal Republic. The Congress and several state legislatures have passed unconstitutional laws aimed at the Communist party, but have failed to prepare legislation which would make *all* subversive conspiracies felonious. Until such time as responsible legislation is written, citizens are protected only by the social pressures which can be developed through the internal discipline of voluntary associations, unions, churches and synagogues, and the like.

What is needed affirmatively is the cultivation of a new and more vigorous style of Christian citizenship.[3] A major contribution of the religious bodies to the integrity of the society would be the recovery of internal integrity and standards of membership—a matter long neglected in the social establishments popularly called "churches." Well-informed and loyal Christians do not become disciplined members of totalitarian conspiracies. They both defend and practice the style of open-faced public discussion. Their conversation about matters of ultimate concern is set in the religious covenant, not in the context of the party. They are guided by the compassionate understanding which informs the words of the Book of Common Prayer, when we pray "for those to whom we have in God's name entrusted the ordinance of government." They produce members of government who are neither thieves nor traitors.

At the present time the major crisis in government centers in the federal Congress, and, to a lesser extent, in some state legislatures, where persons under discipline in totalitarian conspiracies are allowed to sit and also to use their offices to further actions destructive of the law of the land. No Communists or members of the John Birch Society should be suffered in government—in legislatures, especially not in police forces or military command, certainly not in such sensitive offices as those of attorney generals, senators, or governors. But it is in the Congress that the veritable center of national spiritual and political stagnation is located. The Congress has shown itself incapable of establishing a meaningful code of ethics, unable to eliminate common thievery and graft among its members; it is infiltrated

[3] Cf. *The Church and the Body Politic* (Seabury Press, 1969), ch. VII.

by agents disloyal to the common law, the Constitution, and due process of law. In strengthening the middle ground, it is imperative that Christian voters call upon the Republican and Democratic parties to exclude those disloyal to party standards and support only those candidates who are free of ideological taint and subversive discipline.

For the loyal Christian citizen, membership in or fellow-traveling with caucuses and conspiracies of a totalitarian type should be enough in itself to disqualify any person from holding public office. And it should go without saying that no person under ideological revolutionary discipline to communism or fascism or racism can be a member in good standing in a Christian church.

IV

------◆◆◆◆◆◆------

The Middle Ground

◆◆◆◆◆◆◆◆◆◆◆◆◆◆◆◆◆◆◆◆◆◆◆◆◆◆◆◆◆◆◆◆

Demagogue or Dialogue

*I*N ancient Greece there were two schools of thought and two methods of training young men for public life.

One school, the Sophists, held that there was no ultimate truth—merely a motley assortment of many particular "truths." Their pupils were taught to take any case and to win by any means. The legitimate fruit of this school of thought was the demagogue, the popular and facile sloganizer who had so mastered the art of verbal deception that he could turn listeners' heads and hearts away from the real issue. This he frequently accomplished by flinging slogans which appealed to prejudice and by falsely attacking the persons arguing other points of view. There is a minor strain of sophistry prevailing even yet in some modern universities, particularly in occasional departments of speech, theology, law, and education where clever methods of advocacy are exalted and the search for truth deprecated. Much more, the totalitarian parties and systems exalt the demagogue—the glib-tongued orator and facile dialectician who can make a bad case look good by cleverly manipulating popular confusion.

Another school, the Platonic Academy, held that there was truth and that it was ultimate—but that any single mortal could have only a partial and imperfect grasp of it. The pupils of the academy were taught to seek that truth in dialogue with others, for out of a good discussion will come insights and perceptions superior to what any individual started with. Such dialogue must be based on two fundamental premises: one, that the discussion is not idle conversation but in earnest concern and quest for the truth; two, that each participant have respect for the dignity and integrity of others involved. The style of the dialogue has been "baptized" into some churches' emphasis upon congregational and lay participation in decision-making. The dialogue is also deeply lodged in the English and American constitutional tradition of popular government, by which each citizen has a right to participate in making the decisions which affect his present and future.

The extremists are spiritual offspring of the Sophists, as revealed by their hostility to open-faced discussion and their efforts to assassinate the character of those who disagree with them. Moreover, they are not in good faith in the meeting: they arrive replete with hidden agenda, slogans to confuse the issue, mastery of the organizational weapon to effect a "take-over." They broadcast to the rest of us from a soundproof

room, and it speedily becomes evident that they cut
out any facts which might contradict the bad case they
have made on their own. The Communist in the labor
union or peace organization, and the John Bircher in
the PTA or medical society operate in precisely the
same way, to the destruction of the full, free, and informed discussion by which most of us have learned
to learn from each other and from the spirit of truth.

Moreover, the extremists spawn the demagogues. To
visit a "for God and country" convention of the John
Birch Society, or one of the political rallies of the
Wallace campaign, or a mob meeting led by Communists operating among students, as well as some of
the "peace" rallies and "civil rights" demonstrations
controlled by left-wing extremists is to invite the same
eerie sense of the emotional power of unprincipled
charismatics. It is not even necessary to understand
the language: precisely the same demonic thrust was
conveyed by Nazi party congresses at Nürnberg a few
years ago, or can now be perceived in pictures and
reports from the mass meetings attending Mao's cultural revolution in mainland China. The speaker is
not so much a leader who responsibly confronts fellow
citizens with issues for decision—some of them hard
and painful—as he is a spokesman for the mob's hatreds
and frustrations.

The style of the demagogues is ecstatic utterance,
and this is one reason why the political demagogue
appears so often and appeals so directly to persons of
primitive religious experience. Twirl your car radio dial
any night after 10:30 P.M., when the big 50,000 kilowatt
stations come on. This is the hip season of the day
in America for the religious and political masters of
ecstatic utterance. Many of them confuse religious and

political issues hopelessly. Most of them never finish
a sentence but push on from one verbal ejaculation
to another. Passionate hatred and malice ring through
the confusion, coupled with envy toward leaders of
government, the churches, education. All are reminis-
cent, in an awesome way, of the terrible political speaking which we used to hear over the Berlin *Sender* in
Hitler's time, and which can still be heard addressing
mass meetings in East Berlin, Peking, and Havana.

The sober citizen, remembering that we are in-
structed to honor the neighbor and to pray for those
entrusted in God's name with the ordinance of government, will remember the psalmist's description—

> Each evening they come back,
> howling like dogs
> and prowling about the city.
> There they are, bellowing with their mouths,
> and snarling with their lips—
> for "Who," they think, "will hear us?"
> (Psalm 59:5–7)

And if that citizen has been nurtured in the oral tradition of the hymnal as well as the Psalms, a stanza from
Kipling's "Recessional" will seem apt indeed:

> If, drunk with sight of power, we loose
> wild tongues that have not Thee in awe,
> Such boasting as the Gentiles use
> or lesser breeds without the law:
> Lord God of Hosts, be with us yet,
> Lest we forget, lest we forget!

The demagogues are the "wild tongues," neither fear-
ing God nor respecting man, loyal only to the party
and the party "line." They have no place in the dialogue: they do not believe in it, and they do not practice it. The problem is how to turn them off and out.

The Public Opinion, Responsible Dialogue, and the "Fairness Doctrine"

Among citizens devoted to a wise public policy, based on genuine and informed rational discussion, the defense of a responsible mass media has become of first importance. The extremists have made grave inroads into radio and television.

Since the first licensing of broadcasting stations, Congress and the courts have held that in the ownership and operation of a public utility the public interest must come first. The public interest requires truthful and balanced programming. Out of this concern grew first the doctrine and then the rule requiring that stations provide opportunity for answer to persons and organizations attacked, and this rule has proved very important in checking the unrestrained language and scurrilous attacks of radical right extremists against leaders in education and religion. In the short period of its active existence, the Institute for American Democracy has found the personal attack provision of the fairness doctrine a very useful tool to check the extremists. In many cases, station owners were moved to drop the hate broadcasts altogether after their attention had been called to their content. In others, the requirement that equal time be provided free of charge to the victim was cogent: small revenues were thereby cut in half, and stations that had been careless about the quality of their programming knew that questions would arise at the time they came up for renewal of license.

There was no problem with the big network programs at first: the issue lay with the smaller individual stations, most of which had simply ignored the law requiring that individuals and groups be advised of attack and offered time to answer. Under IAD initiative, backed by volunteer citizens who monitored stations carrying considerable extremist propaganda, these stations began to conform to the law. That is, they did until John Banzhaf, a young layman of the former Evangelical United Brethren Church, won his ruling on anti-cigarette advertising. Mr. Banzhaf won the right of anti-cigarette agencies to have free time on the networks to respond to the advertising of the tobacco companies. The networks didn't give much time, far from "equal time," but still their revenue was threatened. At that point the big networks became highly interested, and—with a kitty of several million dollars collected by the cigarette companies—set their high-powered legal staffs to work to eliminate the fairness doctrine altogether.

The first case was opened in a federal district court in Chicago, far from the court in Washington, D.C., where most "fairness" disputes had been handled, and in an area where the courts are notoriously corrupt. They won the first round, but then at the level of the Circuit Court of Appeals the fairness doctrine of the Federal Communications Commission (FCC) was reaffirmed and the judgment of the lower court set aside. The case is presently being appealed to the Supreme Court, where all the law expertise that money can buy will be mounted to eliminate the FCC rule and save the networks the few minutes a day of anti-cigarette warnings that Mr. Banzhaf's vigorous crusade had won. In the process, the minimal restraint upon radical right broadcasting is put in jeopardy. Considering what we know about the poisonous and cancerous effect of cigarettes (and of fascist propaganda!), there has seldom been a clearer situation where pursuit of profit is put ahead of public health and patriotism.

In point of fact, even before the present suspense, most stations paid little attention to the law except when monitored and required to do so. A certain percentage, perhaps as high as 10 percent, are owned or controlled by persons under radical right discipline or else fellow-traveling with them; these stations have consistently ignored the law. In all of these years, no station—including the viciously racist station in Jackson, Mississippi, monitored by a United Church of Christ team—has ever lost its license. Enforcement of the law has been feeble and haphazard, and now even the law itself is in jeopardy.

The only thing which can bring some order and fair play into the jungle of broadcasting and check the poisonous influence of an estimated *10,000 extremist programs per week* which now fill the airwaves, is an aroused citizenry. (With the possible exception of one station on the West Coast, all of these extremist programs are of fascist rather than Communist bent.) Monitoring teams are needed to tape programs and report to the church agencies, and citizens' action is needed to bring pressure to bear upon Congress and upon the FCC itself to restore balanced programming. This is a minimal goal: ideal would be the elimination of disloyal and subversive propaganda altogether.[1]

Dr. Everett C. Parker, director of communication for the United Church of Christ, has been critically involved in the effort to establish some standards of

[1] On this whole problem, see IAD's pamphlet *How to Fight Air Pollution.*

ethical responsibility in radio and television. A trial case, to get the public interest before the Federal Communications Commission, was that involving station WLBT-TV in Jackson, Mississippi. Station WLBT-TV was carefully monitored by a church team for several weeks during the spring of 1964. In spite of the fact that 47 percent of the station's viewers were black citizens, the station was guilty of excluding blacks from programming, failing to use courtesy titles for blacks, bias against blacks in civil rights cases, devotion to segregation and resistance to laws and judicial decisions protecting black citizens in their constitutional rights. After debating for more than a year, the commission majority denied standing to the United Church of Christ and its petitioners and routinely renewed the license of a station contemptuous of a large proportion of its public and disloyal to the law of the land.[2]

During forty years the FCC has never denied a license renewal for cause. It is a well-known principle that failure to enforce law is a chief source of illegality and criminality, and nowhere is this more certain than in the area of the mass media. Until civil initiative is aroused to the point that the Federal Communications Commission represents the public interest, and not merely the financial interests of the industry, radio and television will remain a jungle. The mass media are a jungle in terms of aesthetics and programming judgment, as the resignation of Fred Friendly as president of CBS News again documented: at a time when national political life hung on the Vietnam War, he was

---

[2] Send for the pamphlet of the Office of Communication, United Church of Christ: "How to Protect Citizen Rights in Television and Radio," published in 1968, and available from the office at 289 Park Avenue South, New York, N.Y. 10010.

unable to get the hearings of the Senate Foreign Relations Committee televised instead of a rerun of "I Love Lucy"![3] In terms of curbing extremist broadcasting and maintaining balanced programming—and the matter of pushing subversive politics is more serious in the immediate sense than low-grade aesthetics!—it is clear that neither the industry nor the FCC which defers to it will do the job without greatly increased public pressure. If there is money to be made pushing political pornography, and the FCC assists the industry in getting away with it, the legal requirement that the public service be given priority will be ignored with impunity.

Within this jungle, political adventurers and witch doctors operate with both freedom and profit. The answer is for church groups to organize monitoring committees, to demand equal time under the fairness doctrine, to pressure congressmen to see to it that the FCC fulfills its mandate, and to organize loyal groups of citizens to apply for licenses now held by station managements contemptuous of their ethical and political responsibility.[3]

This is the Age of the Laity in the churches and the age of self-government in the political order. The fact that the Muslim world, sections of state-church Christendom, and the ideological states of communism and fascism have not progressed to such level makes the preservation and strengthening of the basic liberties and dignity of the human person all the more vital.

The cornerstone of our concern is the conviction that every one of God's creatures, the human person

[3] David Manning White and Richard Averson, eds., *Sight, Sound, and Society* (Boston: Beacon Press, 1968), p. 14.

and his most precious communities (church and synagogue, college and university, family and vocational
group), is entitled to participate fully in making the
decisions that govern his present and his future. To
strengthen and advance the dialogue, those pathological
and totalitarian groups and parties which ignore its
rules and—when triumphant—revert to the old rule of
the knife must be muted and destroyed. Done in time,
through church discipline and maintaining constitutional due process against the enemies of orderly change
and growth, the path of moderation and reason can
be broadened and made smooth. Delayed action, coming too late to be effective, is the assistance which the
leftist and rightist totalitarians hope for from an apa-
thetic people.

The greatest gift to the totalitarians is religious and
political indifference and apathy. At the last judgment
the balcony-sitter may plead, "I never harmed a fly."
But the Judge will say, "The fly that you never harmed
carried the plague to millions."

Appendices

1. A Bonhoeffer Fragment
2. Extremist Newspapers and Magazines
3. Checklist of Reliable Sources of Information and Assistance
4. Basic Bibliography on Social Pathology
5. Author's List of Papers on Totalitarianism
6. Totalitarianism (from *Weltkirchenlexikon*)
7. The Methodist Federation for Social Action
8. Film Review: Communism, Extremism, Totalitarianism

1. A Bonhoeffer Fragment *

LOOK AT THE little assistant in the public park: a lov-
able, harmless, well-meaning comrade among his own—
perhaps also a good, true, average father of a family. But
he is a devil at the point where the appeal of his laughable
little power tickles him, and at the same time a crawling
worm before his boss. There are many vices, but none that
brings more misery for human beings than the misuse of
power, and that exactly at the hands of little people. Again
and again history brings forth great abusers of power;
they bring up great opposing power and almost never es-
cape their due judgment; they are demi-gods, who are
not subject to an ordinary human condemnation. They
rise and fall in a few years; but the little abusers of power
never die out. . . . It is the little abusers of power who
lead a people to destruction from within. . . .
Therefore . . . one may not allow himself to be dis-
couraged by the apparent hopelessness of the struggle.
Whoever succeeds in eliminating one of these little tyrants
may take pride in having saved many lives; he is a hero
of humanity, whether anyone else knows it or not. Many
well-meaning people of our class have accustomed themselves to laugh at these petty criminals, and to hold those
for fools who have declared war to the death against them.
This laughter is as foolish and irresponsible as laughter
about a tiny measure of bacteria. . . .

* From fragments of a novel left by Dietrich Bonhoeffer during his imprisonment at the Tegel. The novel, semi-autobio-
graphical, was to tell the story of two families who taught
Christian responsibility to their children, who therefore found
themselves compelled to stand against the popular cult. Published as "Glück und Macht," in the Berlin magazine *Unterwegs*
(1954), No. 4, pp. 196–205. (Translated by F. H. L.)

2. Extremist Newspapers and Magazines

ALTHOUGH NOT COMPLETE, the following list is selected to assist students of social pathology. Certain items are included because they are more apt to be familiar than others, or because they represent organizations or parties more frequently asked about. Other items are included because, although comparatively unknown, they illustrate in striking fashion the pathological posture. A few have been selected because, although they are ostensibly "independent," they in fact whirl in orbit about one of the totalitarian centers of disciplined action.

The most difficult, and sometimes precarious, task of all is to identify "fellow-traveling" magazines or organizations. Yet this must be undertaken, for just as basic to totalitarian strategy as training revolutionary cadres is the misuse of supposedly innocent journals, organizations, and campaigns. Such instruments function as a halfway house to recruit persons who would be frightened away if they knew at once that they were the target of conspiratorial and subversive parties. Just as important, they provide a more antiseptic way of feeding the party line on various issues into the public discussion. Individuals who would immediately suspect an interpretation of, for example, the civil rights movement if it were directly presented by the Communist party or the John Birch Society are less wary if they read the "line" in *The Partisan* of "Youth Against War and Fascism" or *Human Events*.

The extremists, whose strategy is directed toward polarizing political opinion and destroying the middle ground, have a simple operation: if Communist or Communist-oriented, they simply write off all liberal or progressive or conservative individuals and groups as *"bourgeois,"* "agents of colonialism and imperialism," "Wall Street lackeys"; if fascist or fascist-oriented, they simply write off all liberal or progressive or conservative individuals and groups as "comsymps," "soft on communism," "agents of the liberal-socialist-Communist conspiracy." For those of moderate views and measured judgment, however, the problem of identifying journals and organizations which are not what they seem is more difficult: if they are honestly and open-facedly liberal or conservative, they are as entitled as any other to participate in the public discussion—even though we don't like their opinions. Nevertheless, it is imperative to distinguish "conservative" from fascist, "liberal" from Communist. The totalitarians make this task difficult for their own reasons, preferring to hide behind literary and organizational masks rather than to show their true faces. The John Birch Society, although it professes to be engaged in "politics," in fact engaged in a determined drive for power in the Republican Convention of 1964 and in the Wallace campaign of 1968, and it now has under discipline a determined minority of the present Congress.

The difficulty of careful appraisal is illustrated by the method employed in the newspaper and magazine checklist prepared at the University of Michigan—*From Radical Left to Extreme Right* (ed. by Robert H. Muller, 1967). This is a very useful listing, but because of the implicit selection procedure followed (an opinion scale from left to right) a number of journals are included which are not pathologically oriented. More serious, some journals are termed "liberal" (*i.e.*, p. 79, *The Social Questions Bulletin*) or "conservative" (*i.e.*, p. 103, *The American Mercury*; p. 150, *The Wanderer*) which are in fact far from being that innocent.

Certain technical terms are inevitable in any specialized field. In the politics of pathological movements, there are a few indispensable and esoteric terms. "Fellow-traveling" is to follow a "line" fixed by someone else in another place, while pretending to integrity—and independence of discussion and decision. A "front," which may be an honest organization captured and subverted or a phony organization secretly set up and run from behind the scenes, is an organizational campaign or association which in fact serves party interests. "Innocents" are those who are taken in by the "front" and naïvely suppose it to be what it seems. A good many self-styled "liberals" have been "innocents" within instruments controlled by the Communists; in the last three decades, as Dr. Ralph Lord Roy showed in his definitive study, *Communism and the Churches* (New York, 1966), thirty-one or thirty-two Protestant clergymen have been consistent "fellow-travelers." This is nowhere near the "more than 5000" that J. B. Mathews, a renegade fellow-traveler who became a professional spokesman for the radical right, talked about. It is still, however, thirty-one or thirty-two too many.[1] More important right now, it is far from the center of present danger: the radical right. The number of churchmen who today "fellow-travel" with pathological movements of the left is infinitesimal in comparison with the number who presently are drawn into the vortex of fascist-type conspiracies. This goes far beyond such obvious cases as "ministers" of uncertain standing who serve the Ku Klux Klan, White Citizens' Councils, John Birch Society, and such, to "innocents" who get drawn into such political actions as recently inspired by the "United Methodist Laymen" or the "Clergymen's Committee on China."

We do not say, with the fascists, that all liberal clergymen who have foolishly signed Communist-inspired petitions or sponsored Communist-controlled organizations are "comsymps" or conspirators. Neither do we say, with the Communists, that clergymen who have let their names be used by the China Lobby or TACT (a "front" of the John Birch Society) are "fascists." Nor do we join those black ideologues who call Dr. S. I. Hayakawa a "racist" because he is trying by tough measures to pull together

[1] Cf. Appendix 7 for summary on a once-valid Methodist social-action organization which was "captured" for a time and uncritically followed the Communist line.

and save an institution polarized and ravaged between left and right, an assignment made very difficult not only by the extremists but by several years of administrative incompetence before he took charge. On the other hand, we do accept the responsibility of identifying cases where "innocents" have shown persistently poor judgment in picking their associations.

In the final analysis the free society, in contrast to the police state, is held together in good part by trust. In the last instance, we prefer to trust churchmen and educational leaders with names and faces, reputable ordinations and honest degrees. Those who have shown a habit of bad judgment cannot be trusted as fully as those who have been sound of mind and heart. And those whose "fellow-traveling" with the totalitarian left and right has shown a pattern of consistency across years are little different from party members as credible witnesses.

Robert H. Muller of the University of Michigan has provided a very full checklist of information, *From Radical Left to Extreme Right*, which can be used for great detail. A few representative items to be recommended to study groups are the following:

RADICAL LEFT

Bulletin of International Socialism ("Fourth International")
    243 E. 10th Street, NYC 10003 $2.00 per year
Free Student   (pro-Castro, pro-Vietcong)
    2300 Broadway, NYC 10024 $5.00 per year
Insurgent   (W.E.B. DuBois Clubs)
    954 McAllister St., San Francisco, Cal. 94115
                                            $1.25 per year
The National Guardian   ("editor-in-exile," Cedric Belfrage)
    197 E. 4th St., NYC 10009 $7.00 per year
People's World   (ACP)
    81 Clementine St., San Francisco, Cal. 94105
                                            $5.00 per year

The Worker   (ACP)
Box 28, Madison Square Station, NYC 10010
$7.00 per year

RACIST

The Citizen   (White Citizens' Councils)
315-25 Plaza Bldg., Jackson, Miss. 39201
$3.00 per year
Common Sense
530 Chestnut St., Union, N.J. 07083 $3.00 per year
Mohammed Speaks
Mohammed's Mosque #2, 634 E. 79th St., Chicago,
Ill. 60619 $5.20 per year
The Cross and the Flag   (Christian Nationalist Crusade)
P.O. Box 27895, Los Angeles, Calif. 90027
$2.00 per year

RADICAL RIGHT

American Opinion   (John Birch Society)
Belmont, Mass. 02178 $10.00 per year
Christian Anti-Communist Crusade   (Fred Schwarz)
P.O. Box 890, Long Beach, Calif. 90801
Christian Beacon   (Carl McIntire)
756 Haddon Ave., Collingwood, N.J. $2.00 per year
Christian Crusade   (Billy James Hargis)
2808 S. Sheridan Rd., Tulsa, Oklahoma 74102
$2.00 per year
The Herald of Freedom   (Frank A. Capell)
P.O. Box 3, Zarephath, N.J.
Dan Smoot Report
P.O. Box 9538, Lakewood Station, Dallas, Tex.
$10.00 per year
Human Events
410 1st St. S.E., Washington, D.C. 20003
Liberty Letter   (Liberty Lobby)
300 Independence Ave. S.E., Washington, D.C. 20003

Life Line   (H. L. Hunt)
   4330 N. Central Expressway, Dallas, Texas 75206
                                        $5.00 per year
Manion Forum   (Clarence Manion)
   St. Joseph Bank Bldg., South Bend, Indiana
                                        $5.00 per year
On Target   (Minutemen)
   P.O. Box 172, Independence, Mo. $5.00 per year
The Wanderer
   128 E. 10th St., St. Paul 1, Minn.

3. Checklist of Reliable Sources of Information and Assistance

Freedom Institute
Iowa Wesleyan College
Mount Pleasant, Iowa 52641

National Conference of Christians and Jews
43 East 57th Street
New York, N.Y. 10019

Center for the Study of Democratic Institutions
Box 4068
Santa Barbara, Calif. 93103

Hoover Institution on War, Revolution, and Peace
Stanford University
Stanford, Calif. 94305

Research Institute on Communist Strategy and Propaganda
University of Southern California
Los Angeles, Calif. 90007

National Congress of Parents and Teachers
700 N. Rush Street
Chicago, Ill. 60611

Anti-Defamation League
315 Lexington Avenue
New York, N.Y. 10016

American Civil Liberties Union
156 5th Avenue
New York, N.Y. 10010

National Education Association
1201 16th Street, N.W.
Washington, D.C.

American Jewish Committee
165 East 56 Street
New York, N.Y. 10022

National Council of Churches
Information Service
475 Riverside Drive
New York, N.Y. 10027

National Association for Mental Health
10 Columbus Circle
New York, N.Y. 10019

Institute for American Democracy
1330 Massachusetts Ave., N.W.
Washington, D.C. 20005

Group Research Inc.
1404 New York Ave., N.W.
Washington, D.C. 20005

4.   Basic Bibliography on Social Pathology

CONTEMPORARY TOTALITARIAN IDEOLOGIES and systems afford the most serious threat to Western civilization since the rise of Islam over a millennium ago. And so far—to fill out the quota of opening generalizations—there is very little evidence that most responsible leaders of church and campus have in this country begun to give the problem any consistent thought or attention. With all of the vast variety of research in our burgeoning institutions of higher education, we have in America nothing comparable to the *Institut für Zeitgeschichte* in Munich, the excellent documentaries of the *Bundeszentrale für Heimatdienst* in Bonn.

Admittedly, those on the middle European frontier are closer to the challenge than most of us. Nevertheless, the problem is much more acute in some parts of the United States than we sometimes dare to admit. And, with witch doctors and adventurers milking the Americans of millions of dollars annually, the time certainly has come for leaders in the churches and on the campuses to take some responsible initiative in analyzing the problem of totalitarianism and developing strategies and methods to meet it. At the present time, with the exception of a small program at St. Louis University, and somewhat more extensive institutes at UCLA, MIT, Santa Barbara, and Columbia University, there is no place where an interdisciplinary staff is carrying on the research and writing which alone can provide a secure base for meeting and overcoming the totalitarian movements elsewhere than on the battlefield.

If we consider the fact that irresponsible tracts such as Evetts Haley's *A Texan Looks at Lyndon* (Canyon, Texas: Palo Curo Press, 1964), Phyllis Schlafley's *A Choice Not an Echo* (Alton, Ill.: Pere Marquette Press, 1964), and

John A. Stormer's *None Dare Call It Treason* (Florissent, Mo.: Liberty Bell Press, 1964), are distributed by the millions, the magnitude of our neglect of the issue comes into focus. Other church and educational leaders have failed, and still fail, to take the Communist and fascist perils seriously. The American people are left, therefore, in their civic forums and in their churches, either to the tender mercies of those who would exploit and capitalize on their anxieties, or to a blind faith in the integrity and purpose of our national leadership in making decisions beyond the information or comprehension of an uninformed public.

THE MARKS OF TOTALITARIANISM

There is now available a fairly extensive shelf of serious studies of totalitarianism, on the basis of which it is possible to distinguish honest conservatism (however hard-headed) from fascism and honest liberalism (however idealistic) from communism. This distinction is fundamental, and candor compels the admission that neither self-styled "liberals" nor self-styled "conservatives" have always been careful to draw the line. Nevertheless, it can be drawn—as precisely as between measles and scarlet fever.

Monograph studies of special problems, as well as scientific articles, are now fairly numerous. For example, Volume XII of a series of forty-two titles being prepared under the *Kommission zur Geschichte des Kirchenkampfes im nationalsozialistischer Zeitalter* has just been published by Vandenhoeck and Ruprecht of Göttingen. There is no comparable series being assigned and written on the experience with communism, but documents and articles and book notices appear regularly in such newsletters and journals as *Religion in Communist Dominated Areas* (NCCC), *Ost-Probleme* (Bonn), *Hinterden Eisernen Vorhang* (Free Europe Committee), and *Problems of Communism* (USIA).

The listing of bibliographical notices is a fairly heavy

burden for a public, and necessarily semi-popular, lecture
to carry—in contrast to a seminar situation, where the in-
structor deals with a "captive audience." We have tried
to cope with this in part by developing a fairly extensive
"Bibliography on Totalitarianism" (including sections on
communism, Nazism and fascism, American nativism),
built up in a graduate seminar on totalitarianism which
has been given annually for several years. This extensive
Bibliography is available from the Freedom Institute, Iowa
Wesleyan College, Mt. Pleasant, Iowa 52641.

Basic books which have laid the foundations for the
scientific study of totalitarian ideologies, movements, and
systems include the following:

ADORNO, T. W., *The Authoritarian Personality* (New
York: Harper & Brothers, 1950). This is a study of the
personality type which finds closed systems congenial,
even psychologically necessary. Eric Hoffer's *The True
Believer* (New York: Mentor Books, 1951) is a more
popular paperback dealing with the same problem. Not
incidentally, these studies expose the peculiar ambivalence of the fanatic, to whom "the party" becomes a
church, a fellowship of salvation, so that he can swing
from communism to fascism (or vice versa) and back
again. It also lays bare the spiritual crisis of the apostates, who remain "half-men" when they manage to
break away. Arthur Koestler's autobiographical novels
are among the most moving portrayals of the wilderness
into which the heretic, renegade, or apostate must go
forth if he breaks from the "true church" (the party)
which alone carries the meaning of history. Among documentaries, Whittaker Chambers' *Witness* (New York:
Random House, 1952) should also be noted here, along
with Richard Crossman's edition of six personal testimonies of former Communists: *The God that Failed*
(New York: Harcourt, Brace & Co., 1951).

ARENDT, HANNAH, *The Origins of Totalitarianism* (New
York: Harcourt, Brace & Co., 1951), expanded revised

paperback edition (Cleveland: Meridian, 1963). Dr. Arendt shows in her study that anti-Semitism is endemic to the totalitarian theory and practice. The reason for this, which goes far beyond simple matters of prejudice and intolerance (and cannot really be met at all by "educating for tolerance"), is the fact that the Jew—whether he is a man of faith or not—is by his very existence a representative of the Author of history whom the totalitarian ideologues deny. Both Stalin and Hitler were bitter anti-Semitics, and they collaborated, for example, in the destruction of the Warsaw Ghetto. Under temptation and pressure, the gentiles can revert to tribalism and racism. The baptized Catholics and Protestants of Germany regress to Teutonic folkways. The baptized Catholics and Orthodox of Russia and eastern Europe go back to pan-Slav mysticism (cf. Cornelius Krahn: "Russia: Messianism-Marxism," XXXI *The Journal of Bible and Religion* (1963) 3:210–15). Anti-Semitism, in its modern political manifestations, is a legitimate offspring of the same declining culture-religion ("Christendom") which spawns the false political religions (cf. Jules Isaac: *Has Anti-Semitism Roots in Christianity?* New York: NCCJ, 1961). It is difficult to give this dimension of the totalitarian threat its proper due without reference to such artistic treatment of the horrors of "the final solution to the Jewish problem" as Andre Schwarz-Bart's *The Last of the Just* (New York: Bantam Books, 1962) or Alexander Donat's *The Holocaust Kingdom* (New York: Holt, Rinehart & Winston, 1963).

It is perhaps worth mentioning that the magazine, *The Thunderbolt*, which calls upon the mob to rise up and defend "Christian America" by killing the Jews, is openly sold by street corner peddlers in Chicago's Loop. It is no accident that the rise of fascist movements in the Deep South should be accompanied by the bombing of synagogues, that Robert Shelton of the KKK should condemn the civil rights movement as a "Jew plot." It is no accident that when one of the few enlightened men left in the parliament of the Union of South Africa arose a few months ago to protest the new round of repressive measures enforced by that fascist government, back-bench members of the *Broederbund* (the conspiracy which actually controls that unhappy land), should bury his words in a noisy chant, "Finkelstein! Kinkelstein!"

Anti-Semitism is one of the earliest seismographic readings on incipient totalitarian movements. Long before they have the effrontery to attack the constitution and law of a land, before the policies to repress the churches are adopted, their denial of the God of Abraham, Isaac, and Jacob—who is also the Christians' God if they do not apostatize, and take on protective coloration—is borne by the Jews. Nothing could emphasize more clearly the importance of the Christian-Jewish dialogue and cooperation to strengthen justice and law in the open society.

EBENSTEIN, WILLIAM, *Today's Isms: Communism, Fascism, Capitalism and Socialism* (New York: Prentice Hall, 1954). Professor Ebenstein, formerly of Princeton and now at the University of California, Santa Barbara, has become one of America's leading authorities on the Communist and fascist movements and systems. He has conducted summer institutes in the field. His manual, *Totalitarianism* (New York: Holt, Rinehart & Winston, 1962), is one of the best study books for any adult study group.

FRIEDRICH, CARL J., ed., *Totalitarianism* (Cambridge: Harvard University Press, 1954), now available in paperback (New York: Universal Library, 1962). Professor Carl Friedrich, of the Littauer Center at Harvard, is perhaps the leading American political scientist to study and publish in this field. He was responsible for a national Conference on the Nature of Totalitarianism held at the American Academy (Boston, 1953), and the essays in this volume derive from that series of sessions. Bertram Wolfe, the late Waldemar Gurian of Notre Dame, Hannah Arendt, William Henry Chamberlin, and many other experts wrote for the occasion. Dr. Friedrich also has published other essays and books in the field, notably a study of the Soviet power structure done with one of his students: C. J. Friedrich and Z. K. Brzizenski, *Totalitarian Dictatorship and Autocracy* (New York: F. I. Praeger paperback, 1964). Brzizenski, now a professor at Columbia, has conducted institutes on the problem of communism, has published books of his own, and is one of our leading authorities on conditions and developments in the Soviet bloc. Cf. *The Permanent Purge: Politics in Soviet Totalitarianism* (Cambridge: Harvard University Press, 1956) and *The Soviet Bloc: Unity and Conflict* (New York: F. I. Praeger paperback, 1961).

LEWIS, JASZI and JOHN D., *Against the Tyrant* (Glencoe: Free Press, 1957). This book is a study of one of the classical problems of the political conscience: when and under what circumstances to resist, even to slay, the tyrant. The problem assumes particular significance in the modern period of popular sovereignty, where every citizen shares to some degree in the responsibility for government policy. It becomes acute in the light of the doctrine established by the International Tribunals at Nürnberg, to the effect that even a military officer is obligated to disobey and/or to resist commands which he knows to be immoral and contrary to the *jus gentium*. This was the specific issue faced by the martyrs, including Dietrich Bonhoeffer, Father Delp (S.J.), and Graf Helmuth von Moltke, and we now have the documents on their inner and outer struggle. Cf. Helmut Gollwitzer, et al., ed., *Dying We Live: The Final Message and Records of the Resistance* (New York: Pantheon Books, 3d ed., 1961).

In terms of the right of resistance itself, important books are Arthur Cochrane's *The Church's Confession Under Hitler* (Philadelphia: Westminster Press, 1962); Gordon Zahn's *German Catholics and Hitler's War* (New York: Sheed & Ward, 1962); Richard Solberg's *God and Caesar in East Germany* (New York: Macmillan Co., 1961); John Conway's *The Nazi Persecution of the Churches* (New York, Basic Books, 1968). On the matter of the attempted overthrow of Hitler and Nazism, July 20, 1944, much has been published. Especially useful is a small volume of court testimonies in connection with the 1951 trial of Major General Remer, the officer who commanded the *Gross-Deutschland* battalion which put down the revolt in Berlin, who later attempted to lead a new-Nazi comeback in the *Bundesrepublik* until both Nazi and Communist political conspiracies were ruled out of the public forum by law. Cf. Herbert Kraus, ed., *Remerprozess . . . Gutachten nebst Urteil* (Hamburg: Giarardet & Co., 1953).

In the German situation, as today in Soviet Russia, no effective internal resistance can occur without the assistance of the military. John W. Wheeler-Bennett's *The Nemesis of Power* (New York: St. Martin's Press, 1954) shows the moral deterioration of the German military profession, which finally made it impossible for a resistance to be successful. At the critical juncture, General Beck (Berlin) and General von Kluge (Paris) could have saved the day even when Von Stauffenberg's attempt failed to kill the Führer: both of them suffered a complete paralysis of decision. This should, among other things, cause us to read John M. Swomley's *The Military Establishment* (Boston: Beacon Press, 1964) with special care. Eventually, perhaps, with the skills in nonviolent direct action which are being developed, it may be possible to build a new warfare without violence and thereby a path along which popular overthrow of totalitarian systems is possible. Today that is not the case, and it tolls the bell for Jeffersonian and Wilsonian views of national self-determination.

TALMON, J. H., *The Origins of Totalitarian Democracy* (London: Secker & Warburg, 1952) and *Political Messianism: The Romantic Phase* (London: Secker & Warburg, 1960) are two volumes of a continuing study by a professor at Hebrew University. Dr. Talmon's thesis is that since the French Revolution popular government has developed in two directions. First, there is the continuing tradition—chiefly found in the Anglo-Saxon constitutional systems—of pedestrian, non-apocalyptic, problem-solving government. This form of government is "secular" (*i.e.*, without strenuous religious overtones or commitments), limited, theologically speaking "creaturely." Government is regarded, in the Judaeo-Christian sense, as a necessary evil: because of the fall, and man's sin, great concentrations of unchecked power must be avoided. Second, there is the strain out of which modern dictatorships have developed—all claiming, in some sense, to represent "the will of the people." Based on an essentially optimistic view of human nature and its potential, they sustain systems which carry heavy apocalyptic overtones. The party which "educates the masses" becomes, for an inner circle, a substitute for church or synagogue. The Communist "vanguard" or fascist "elite" represents a secularized perversion of the biblical "elect people." It is the carrier and revealer of the real meaning of history. By a process of apotheosis, the party heroes become "saints" of the movement; the masses are encouraged to make pilgrimage to their shrines (Lenin, Horst Wessel). All history moves toward a day of consummation and reckoning: "der Tag," "the revolution," "the final conflict," when the secret truth will be revealed as the basis for a fundamental reordering of all life.

The present loyal nuclei are cut loose from continuity and tradition, to be the "new man" or "superman" of the new age. In its mature stages, a "secularized cultus" is developed—as can be studied with considerable exactitude in the party rites of "baptism" (name-giving), "confirmation" (*Jugendweihe*), marriage, and burial.

Politics under ideological impress represents a regression to "sacral" societies, to the use of all instruments—public education, business, government, welfare organizations, trade unions, and the like—to effect a total and essentially "religious" objective. As Ernst Cassirer pointed out in his brilliant volume, *The Myth of the State* (New Haven: Yale University Press, 1946, p. 275): "One of the principal aims and fundamental conditions of the totalitarian state is the principle of *Gleichschaltung*. In order to subsist it has to eliminate all other forms of social and cultural life and efface all distinctions." He also pointed out that this all-encompassing, monistic, perfect "state" is impossible to the Christian. "The state could be justified to a certain extent, but it could never be rendered beautiful. It could not be conceived as pure and immaculate; for it always bore the mark of its origin. The stigma of the original sin was indelibly branded on it. That makes the sharp differences between classical Greek, and early Christian thought" (p. 109). The Christian citizen today in America opposes all efforts to revert to "sacral" society: he knows that secular government is the necessary corollary to his liberties—especially religious liberty.

At this point special attention should also be called to a specialized study which contributed several important points to the understanding of totalitarianism: W. Chalupa's *Rise and Development of a Totalitarian State* (Leiden: H. E. Stenfort Kroese N. V., 1959). Dr. Chalupa's study is concentrated on the Communist takeover in Czechoslovakia, which—like that in Poland and many other areas—was effected by the skillful subversion of a coalition government. The Communists have perfected that combination of secret terror and public probity which marks totalitarians generally. It is not an accident, but by deliberate tactic, that at the very time John Rousselot is trying to create a public image of decency and propriety for the John Birch Society, the hatchetmen of the movement should be launching the "Dial-a-Lie" program, the telephone service called "Let Freedom Ring!" The totalitarians, in perfecting *the organizational weapon* (cf. the study by that name by Phillip Selzwick: McGraw-Hill, 1952), are specialists in destroying united fronts and coalition governments. The moral is clear, whether we are speaking of Viet Nam or Cuba or the free speech movement on American campuses: any cooperation with Communists or fascists presumes on their part a good faith toward the dialogue which does not exist.

Among the studies of pre-totalitarian conditions in the United States which are available, one of the most significant is James W. Silver's *Mississippi: The Closed Society* (New York: Harcourt, Brace & World, 1964). The parallels to suppression of liberty and self-government in Germany's Third Reich, in Russia, and the Union of South Africa are striking, and make it obvious that only the federal presence has prevented some state machines from going fascist altogether.

WHOM DO YOU BELIEVE?

The issue resolves itself, like every matter of judicious decision, to a matter of credible sources. Representative Charles A. Vanik of Ohio entered in *The Congressional Record* (88th Congress, 2d session; Vol. 110, No. 173, pp. A 4650–64) no less than forty-two points where the Stormer tract misinterprets, misquotes, or simply manufactures "evidence," with the conclusion that "the subject book is, at least, an incredibly poor job of research and documentation, and at worst, a deliberate hoax and a fraud." The student who must decide on its credibility is entitled to know that the author is a member of the John Birch Society.

Critical analysis requires careful use of "the historical method." At least since Leopold von Ranke, the student can no longer accept something as true simply because "everyone believes it": he must check the sources, and determine whether the one speaking or writing is a credible witness.

> By careful use of exact quotations, quotation marks, avoidance of the first person singular in writing, identification of sources, and the other comparatively recent techniques of "the historical method," known persons must be brought forward by the historian in order to make a responsible dialogue possible. (F.H.L., "The New Church History," *Bulletin* of the AATS, No. 25, June, 1962, p. 6).

Take an example of one popular "authority" on anti-communism, who weekly broadcasts over more than 130 radio stations. Although he uses both "Reverend" and "Doctor," he holds ordination from no known church and a degree from no accredited institution. His first "degrees" were purchased from "Burton College," condemned by the United States government as a "degree mill." He also acquired "doctors' degrees" from "Belin Memorial University," whose "president" was sent to federal penitentiary for running an interstate fraud, and "Defender Seminary," a letterhead organ of the notorious anti-Semite, Gerald Winrod. His financial activities, which led the government to suspend his "front group" from tax-exempt status, and his "academic" and political manipulations have been extensively studied by psychologists and other qualified research experts. Cf. Arnold Forster and Benjamen R. Epstein: *Danger on the Right* (New York: Random House, 1964), ch. IV.

The truth is that like another well-known spokesman for the radical right, a defrocked preacher who broadcasts over 750 weekly radio broadcasts, our subject is not a credible witness. He would not know a genuine Communist from a Chinese Boxer. But, as his financial success as an agitator shows, he does know a good thing when he sees it!

His biography and "line" have been carefully studied by John H. Redekop in *The American Far Right: A Case Study of Billy James Hargis and Christian Crusade* (Grand Rapids: Wm. B. Eerdmans Publishing Co., 1968).

5. Author's List of Papers on Totalitarianism

1. "Pastoral Care Under Totalitarianism," XIII *Christianity and Crisis* (1953) 4:42f.
2. "The Free Church vs. Totalitarianism," chapter V of *The Free Church* (Boston: Beacon Press, 1957).
3. "The Protestant Churches and Totalitarianism (Germany, 1933–1945)," chapter in Carl J. Friederich, ed., *Totalitarianism* (Cambridge: Harvard University Press, 1954), pp. 108–19. Excerpt with discussion of problematic in Yinger J. Milton, *Religion, Society and the Individual* (New York: Macmillan Co., 1957), pp. 553–55.
4. "Barmen: A Twenty-Fifth Anniversary Tribute," XIX *Christianity and Crisis* (1955) 9:71f.
5. Chapters I–III in Franklin H. Littell, *The German Phoenix* (New York: Doubleday & Co., 1960).
6. "The Importance of the Church Struggle to the Ecumene," in *Franz Lieber Heyte* (Bad Godesberg, 1959), No. 3, pp. 32–45; in German, "Die Bedeutung des Kirchenkampfes für die Oekumene," XX *Evangelische Theologie* (1960) 1:1–21.
7. "Totalitarianism," in Franklin H. Littell, and Hans Hermann Walz, eds., *Weltkirchenlexikon: Handbuch der Oekumene* (Stuttgart: Kreuz-Verlag, 1960); under the sponsorship of the Deutscher Evangelisher Kirchentag. (Cf. appendix 6 to this volume.)
8. "From Barmen (1934) to Stuttgart (1945): The path of the Confessing Church in Germany," XXX *A Journal of Church and State* (1961) 1:41–52.
9. "The Christian Encounter with Totalitarianism," a pamphlet based on an address at Highland Park Methodist Church, Dallas, Texas (April, 1961). Reprinted in XV *The Perkins School of Theology Journal* (1961) 1:24–32.

10. "The Christian Encounter with Totalitarianism," a pamphlet based on an address at Earlham School of Religion, Richmond, Indiana (June 29, 1961).
11. "The Challenge of the Radical Right," XXII *Christianity and Crisis* (1962) 4:38f.
12. "The Church Speaks—or Dies," in *Witness Through Service: the 1963–64 Program Book*, Women's Division of Christian Service (New York: Board of Missions of the Methodist Church, 1963), pp. 62–69.
13. "The Church Struggle in America," *Presbyterian Survey* (1967), 7:19–21, 9:23–25.
14. "The Growing Church Struggle in America," VII *Andover Newton Quarterly* (1967) 3:113–26.
15. "Extremism: Its Threat to Democracy," I *Face* (1968) 2:24–27.
16. "Christians in a Violent Age," VIII *dialog* (1969) 1:33–35.

6.   *Totalitarianism* *

TOTALITARIANISM is the result of the decline of the entire order of life in the Occident and the attempt to achieve an integration of society through coordination of all social functions by the state. It is built on the confidence with which the European nations have greeted the state since the nineteenth century, and it first became possible as a result of modern secularization (see Hegel: the State = earthly god). Beyond that it represents the perversion of concepts and institutions which is characteristic of Europe in a state of crisis. Marx and Engels, Lenin, Stalin and Trotsky, Hitler and Rosenberg, Mussolini, Franco and Perón, all of them, can only be rightly understood in terms of the general crisis of the West in the last two centuries.

Totalitarianism cannot be understood either as the return of an "oriental despotism" or as a more powerful and more forceful form of known despotic type. There are certain likenesses to the bureaucratic centralism of Frederick II or Louis XIV. But the uniqueness of modern totalitarianism is that "the polictical world has lost its connection not only with religion or metaphysics, but also with all the other forms of man's ethical and cultural life. It stands alone—in an empty space" (Cassierer, *The Myth of the State*, p. 140). In the French Revolution especially, the hostility of incipient totalitarianism to independent centers of discussion and organized opinion, to a divided sovereignty, came to the fore in the destruction of the catholic and universal dimension of religious associations and in the artificial construction of a national Cult of Reason. "The general will achieves its purest expression when

* An article by F.H.L. in Franklin H. Littell and Hans Herman Walz, eds., *Weltkirchenlexikon: Handbuch der Oekumene* (Stuttgart: Kreuz-Verlag, 1960), cols. 1466–69. (Trans. F.H.L.)

all citizens confront the state as individuals and are not bound together in lesser associations." With this sentence Rousseau grounded the priority of the state over against all other forms of human association and thereby also laid the foundation for totalitarianism. In the earlier despotisms, in spite of these and other similarities—among which, for the ordinary subject, the resolute contempt for humanity and the human measure was the most important—any asserted claims of the state to omnipotence were checked by other social institutions which in the end displayed great residual strength: the hierarchy and other estates, the emerging commercial and working associations, the papacy, other nation states.

Only in the modern age have Christianity and its institutions lost sufficient authority, and government attained sufficient monolithic control over the instruments of transportation and communication, and military service become sufficiently "proletarianized" (not in the economic but in the classical sense of the word: "in the society but not of it"), for governments to emerge which use the same methods against their own people which they have for long used against colonial subject peoples. That this has been accomplished and maintained with the enthusiastic support of the large majority of those so ruled has been possible not only because of the resolute suppression of all dissent and the means for expressing it, but because of the quasi-religious nature of the totalitarian state. This is the new and unique characteristic of totalitarianism, that the sole instrument of community and coherence left —the state—has become no longer a "higher power to punish evil and protect the good," but itself embodies the divine. In totalitarianism, the state is the carrier of the meaning of history, the center of cultic practices and religious feelings. In this intensively idealistic situation, the state becomes not only the positive enemy of other patterns of association and community (*Gleichschaltung*), but the symbol of a scheme of salvation, the purveyor of a "new Islam" (Barth), and in the end itself the anti-Christ (Bonhoeffer). For the elite, who share in the faith and power of the mystery, totalitarianism is a modern Gnostic religion; for the mass-man, the demand for self-sacrifice for vague and distant purposes has a therapeutic function, saving him from nihilism and self-hate.

The definition of totalitarianism is difficult, for no area of life is left untouched and no social or political or economic or cultural institution is left unchallenged. There have been various forms of totalitarianism in the twentieth century, differing on occasion at significant points. Fascism, Falagism Perónism, the Irish Republican Army, American nativism—all belong to the study; but the most significant objects of research are Nazism and Communism.

In spite of a wide variety of issues, the essential marks of totalitarianism can be summarized as follows: (1) hostility to all sub-political forms of organization, to all divided sovereignty—whether of estates, constitutional federalism, or voluntary associations of discipline (churches, trade unions, universities, professional groups, etc.); (2) hostility to independent centers of public opinion, where full, free, and informed discussion is maintained; (3) hostility to constitutional and representative forms of self-government on a pattern of devotion (Denmark, Switzerland), or in terms of ancient and pre-contractural entities (England, United States); (4) a dynamic and organismic doctrine of the state; (the state = the factor of universal integration in society), with a separation of the vanguard or elite from the followers (see Lenin's *State and Revolution*, Hitler's *Mein Kampf*), with an apocalyptic affirmation of conflict and violence (vs. the harmonism of the nineteenth-century continuum, but also vs. newer syntheses); (5) a program of politics in terms of ultimates, rather than concentrated on the pedestrian and problem-solving practical needs (speculative and "Gnostic" politics); (6) a blending of political with pseudo-religious concepts and goals, in the interpretation and even in the periodization of history. Generically, the emergence of the totalitarian type has been conclusively related to the Platonic and romantic views of the state and to pietism.

Among the problems requiring further research, study, and writing are the following: (1) the abuse and manipulation of parliamentary and democratic instruments to accomplish totalitarian ends; (2) the affinity to war and militarism; (3) the necessity of anti-Semitism; (4) the totalitarian periodization of history, with the emergence of a political Joachimitism, a new Age of the Spirit, a new non-sectarian way, a secularzied primitivism (Lenin on "the withering away of the state"); (5) the hostility to creeds and confessions in *"positives Christentum"*; (6) the possibilities and styles of resistance, including what types of religious and institutional grouping prove most rugged and which are most vulnerable to subversion; (7) the deliberate polarization of the political consensus between right radicalism and left radicalism, with subsequent collapse of the vital center which ensures order and stability; (8) the alliance of totalitarian parties before the seizure of power with anonymous and underworld elements, operating in defiance of due process and without the discipline of open-faced dialogue (*i. e.*, extra-legally).

In the process of studying these and related problems, the essential nature of liberties in the open society is brought to the fore; the integrity of institutions is fairly tested by their staying power under pressure from within and without as well as by their positive contributions.

The struggle with totalitarianism has been conducted especially by the churches, their existence immediately threatened by it. Pope Pius XI condemned totalitarianism in the encyclical *"Mit brennender Sorge"* (3/4/37). In the same year (1937) the Oxford Conference concerned itself with the problem of the total state.

7.   The Methodist Federation for Social Action *

THE PURPOSE of this project is to understand the development and problems of the Methodist Federation for Social Service/Action. In relation to the problems of the Federation an effort will be made to relate what influence the Federation may have had from Russian communism. In particular the influence of two leaders of the Federation, Harry F. Ward and Jack R. McMichael, is to be examined as to whether or not they led the Federation toward Russian communism.

The Methodist Federation for Social Service (MFSS) was founded in 1907. From the beginning it attracted men of unusual ability for relating the Christian Gospel to the social problems of their time. Perhaps the most outstanding was Bishop Francis J. McConnell, for a long time the President of the Federation (until 1944). He and others who formed the Federation knew that the Gospel of Jesus Christ was not an exclusively personal matter; it also had social dimensions of love and justice.

The five churchmen who met to organize the Methodist Federation for Social Service (later, in 1947, the Methodist Federation for Social Action) were Worth M. Tippy, then a pastor in Cleveland; E. Robb Waring of the *Western Christian Advocate*; Frank Mason North of the New York City Society; Bishop Herbert Welch; and Harry F. Ward, the pastor of the Stockyard district in Chicago.

From the beginning the MFSS attracted not only clergymen but social workers. The Federation influenced and

* A cover sheet for the seminar on totalitarianism, Chicago Theological Seminary, Winter 1965–66, by R. W. Younts. (This graduate seminar, now in its tenth year, has produced some dozens of research papers and theses on pathological persons and groups. It is a seminar especially important to Methodists. F.H.L.)

shaped the content of the first social creed from any Protestant Church. (The Methodist Episcopal Church adopted
the first social creed in 1908.) Harry F. Ward of the
MFSS was one of those who helped to frame the Methodist Social Creed of 1908. The Federation always has
been an independent and unofficial group of Methodists.

The first national conference of the Federation was held
in Washington, D. C., on Tuesday, December 3, 1907.
At this conference the delegates adopted the following
statement of purpose (Art. 2 of the Federation Constitution):

> The objects of the Federation shall be to deepen
> within the Church the sense of social obligation and
> opportunity, to study problems from the Christian
> point of view, and to promote social service in the
> spirit of Jesus Christ. (from *Across Social Frontiers,
> the Story of the MFSS, 1907–1947*, by Alson J.
> Smith)

Whereas this statement of purpose is general in nature,
touching upon significant points on learning and service
in the social order, the discussion of economics received
increasing attention over the years. Capitalism became an
intolerable form of economy to the Federation and social
democratic planning for a people's economy came into the
forefront. Thus the Federation pronouncements moved
clearly toward a critical evaluation of American capitalism
while endorsing and encouraging "a planned and planning
social economy." (from *Outline of a Christian Program
for Social Change*—a plan formulated by the MFSS during 1935–36, p. 7–8) Furthermore, "to be successful a
planned social economy must rest upon social ownership
of the resources and plant necessary to its operation."
(*Ibid.*, 1935–36, *Outline*, p. 7–8)

It is evident that Harry F. Ward, who served as secretary of the Federation until 1944, influenced the Federation in the direction of economic considerations. His
sympathy with Russian communism, which espouses an

ownership and control of all property by the people, is obvious in his writing, In 1942, Harry Ward wrote: "In the days of the New Economic Policy (these were five-year programs started by Stalin in 1929) I went to Soviet Russia to find out if the Western world were right in its verdict that this policy meant the return to Capitalism. I judged that Lenin was the one who was right. He said, 'We will take one step backward in order to take two steps forward.' These two steps were taken with Seven-League Boots—the first Five-Year Plan and the collectivization program. In the critical year of these two steps I went again to find out if these two incentives of an infant socialist society were as practical and powerful as those of the capitalist world, and whether their weaknesses and dangers could be overcome as those of capitalism had not been. The evidence showed that the Soviet economy was succeeding and would succeed. Recent developments have provided additional proof." ("Is Russia Forsaking Communism?" *The Christian Century*, 10/28/42, p. 1315–16)

Another Leader of the MFSS, Jack R. McMichael, who had been a student of Harry Ward at Union Theological Seminary in New York, influenced the MFSS in the direction of Russian communism. McMichael was the executive secretary of the MFSS from 1944 to 1953. His indiscriminate support of peace organizations, regardless of whether they were Communist front or not, was an embarrassment and concern to many Federation leaders. Harold DeWolf, professor at Boston School of Theology, asked him to clarify his position with regard to "Stalinist Communism":

> In face of the questions raised by many of the most loyal contributing members of the Federation and respected urging from other officers and associates in the Federation, Mr. McMichael has failed to issue any general systematic critique of the principles and program of Stalinist Communism over his signature. (Letter to executive committee of MFSA, 6/30/50)

McMichael had denied, in 1948, though with no systematic critique of communism, that he was a Communist. In 1947, Franklin H. Littell, who had rejoined the new Executive Committee in 1943 after resigning in protest against Ward's "line" in 1940, again resigned to protest McMichael's political "line."

In 1950, John Mecartney, a student at Garrett Theological Seminary, issued a factual, confidential statement to the executive committee of the MFSA which pointed out the numerous United Front groups to which McMichael had or still had some relationship. McMichael's annual report to the Federation in 1947 stated support of the United Nations and denounced the Truman Doctrine and the Marshall Plan. As the Overstreets show in their book, *What We Must Know about Communism*, this type of denunciation was encouraged in 1947 by the Communist party. Mecartney in his statement says that one of the principles in discerning Communist sympathizers is whether they consistently back Russian policies when they are promulgated. Clearly in this instance, as well as in other cases, McMichael was following the Russian Communist position.

Were McMichael and Ward members of the Communist party? Ralph Lord Roy in his book on *Communism and the Churches* (p. 323) says they were not. There is no clear evidence that they were. However, there is much evidence that indicates both men were, as Roy says, "consistent and determined apologists for the Soviet Union and the world Communist movement" (*Communism and the Churches*, p. 323). Their influence through the Federation publication, *Social Questions Bulletin* and in many meetings where they represented the Federation was sufficient to create realistic proof for their shaping the direction in which the Federation was going. More than any other two men they were in a position to shape the destiny of the Federation for good or ill.

Today the Federation continues to exist but without either the support of many of its capable former members or without much hope of recovery as a creative and contributive organization within or outside the church.

8.   Film Review:
Communism, Extremism, Totalitarianism *

COMMUNISM—GENERAL

"Who Goes There?"

Review the rise of communism from its beginnings in the late seventeenth century to the establishment of the wall between East and West Germany in 1961. Outlines the Communist movement from the humanistic ideals of philosophy in the seventeenth and eighteenth centuries. The basic ideas of Marx and Engels are clearly described. Documents the role of Lenin and Trotsky early in the twentieth century. Follows development of Soviet policy through Khruschev's obtaining power.

2 reels, 52 min.
sh-c-adult
McGraw-Hill $275 ($10 rental)
Indiana University ($9.40 rental)

"The Challenge of Ideas"

Analyzes and discusses the basic values and essential differences between the Communist and democratic political viewpoints. Contrasts the American concept of exploration of truth, of the dignity of man, of the idea of individual liberty, of the right of self-government, with the Communist concept of the individual as a digit of the state. Discusses the cold war and the threat to world peace by the aggressive nature of the Communist states.

* Compiled by The Freedom Institute and the Department of Psychology, Iowa Wesleyan College, Mt. Pleasant, Iowa 52641.

1 reel, 30 min.
sd-h-ad. IFB.
University of Iowa ($5.00 rental)
Indiana University ($4.40 rental)

COMMUNISM—CHINA

"China Under Communism" (Revised Edition)

This documentary is an uncensored, eye-witness report by John Strohm, the first authorized United States newsman permitted to travel in Red China and photograph what he saw. The film shows Communist methods of forcing radical and sweeping changes in traditional patterns of living; describes China's most critical social and economic problems, and considers the possible effects of Communist success in China on world security. This revised edition includes additional information obtained by John Strohm through interviews with scores of refugees from Red China.

1 reel, 22 min.
jh-sc-c-adult
Encyclopedia Britannica Films, Color $265, B/W $135
Iowa State University ($3.25 rental)
Wisconsin State University
Indiana University ($7.65 rental)

"Communist China"

Reports on the progress of communism in China and discusses China's potential power. Pictures efforts to unify the Chinese people through the life and discipline of the communes. Shows the building of industrial plants and attempts to update methods of farming. Points out the use of education as a unifying factor.

1 reel, 23 min.
jh-sh-col-gen.
McGraw-Hill $140 ($10 rental)
Indiana University ($5.15 rental)

"Red China"

Outlines the changes that have taken place in Red China since 1949. Depicts, through these rare and only films known to have been taken since 1958 by a person from a non-Communist country, the life led by the Chinese under Communist rule.

1 reel, 55 min.
sh-col-sp.
McGraw-Hill
Indiana University ($9.40 rental)

COMMUNISM—EASTERN EUROPE

"Hungary and Communism—Eastern Europe In Change"

Dr. Andrew Gyorgy of Boston University, a political scientist and a native of Hungary, introduces the film with some observations about the changes taking place in Hungary. Reveals the span of three generations of one family, with pictorial reminiscences of life in pre-Communist days, Hungary under early Russian domination, and Hungary today. A balanced picture of present-day life in Hungary—cultural, economic, industrial (urban and rural)—is presented showing the subtle and obvious changes that are taking place.

1 reel, 17 min.
1-jh-sh-c-adult
Encyclopedia Britannica Films, color $200, B/W $102.50
Iowa State University ($2.40 rental)

COMMUNISM—USSR

"The Rise of Soviet Power"

With stinging dramatic impact, this adaptation of an original BBC production brings historic events into sharp focus as it demonstrates the Soviet Union's determined drive toward radical domestic change and world domination. Showing the role of successive leaders from revolution to present day, it stresses Lenin's development of the ideological base of state supremacy, the ruthless tactics employed by Stalin in producing industrial, educational, and technological advances, and finally the Khrushchev regime marked by national pride in space race achievements. Today, concludes this forceful film, Russia has moved far forward in power and prestige—yet how her people will choose to use these tools remains an enigma.

2 reels, 61 min.
sh-c-d
BBC
McGraw-Hill $370 ($10 rental).

FASCISM—GENERAL

"Twentieth Century Revolution In World Affairs: The Fascist Revolution"

Examines the fundamental political ideas of fascism: rejection of the individual and deification of the state, distrust of reason and belief in force, and renunciation of freedom in favor of security. Uses documentary film footage to show the environment in which fascism rose in Germany and Italy immediately following World War I, and the disastrous results it brought until its defeat in 1945. Points out that fascism was not necessarily eradicated by World War II.

1 reel, 29 min.
sh-col-gen
NET
Indiana University ($5.40 rental)

FASCISM—NAZI GERMANY

"The Rise And Fall Of The Third Reich"

This powerful television documentary based on William L. Shirer's significant literary achievement features specially-filmed interviews with a number of Hitler's intimates and victims. Rare archive films used throughout all three segments strongly create "you are there" realism.

Write to: Xerox Corporation, P.O. Box 24, Rochester, New York 14603.

"Minister of Hate"

Describes Goebbel's work as Germany's Minister of Propaganda. Includes interviews with film producer Fritz Lang and English historian H. R. Trevor Roper on Goebbel's career as a "super salesman." Illustrates how Goebbels gained complete control of the media and used the raido as his greatest weapon to build up Hitler. Traces his efforts through World War II and climaxes with his suicide.

1 reel, 25 min.
sh-c-gen
CBS
McGraw-Hill
Indiana University ($5.65 rental)

"Adolf Hitler"

Traces the life of the German leader from his early childhood, through his rise to absolute power, to his probable suicide near the end of World War II.

Part I. The Rise of Power. Scans his family background and troublesome youth. Shows the power of his fiery oratory as he manipulated and browbeat his way to dictatorship. Recounts events leading to World War II and the tragic years of the war.

Part II. The Fall of The Third Reich. Shows the decline of German might after the battles of Britain and Stalingrad, and the Allied invasion of Europe. Concludes with the Russian capture of Berlin and evidence indicating Hitler's suicide.

2 reels, 52 min.
jh-sh-col
McGraw-Hill $150 each reel
Indiana University ($9.90 rental, both reels)

EXTREMISM—U.S.A.

"The Red Myth, No. 11: Communism In The U.S."

Traces the history of communism in the United States. Uses dramatic re-enactments of the Bridgeman Convention in 1921 and shows how the Communist party in the United States was controlled by the Communist International. Special guest is Benjamin Gitlow, former general secretary of the Communist party of America and American representative to the Comintern in the 1920's. He tells why he joined and left the Communist party.

1 reel, 29 min.
sh-c-gen
NET
Indiana University ($5.40 rental)

"The Radical Americans: What's New On The Left?"

Draws a distinction between the young radicals and the strong tradition of radicalism in this country, and the dogmatic Communist radicals of the Communist party USA or Progressive Labor, the so-called "pot left." Presents ideas of what the "new left" stands for. Introduces and reveals the views of this movement through the spokesmen of the various "new left" organizations.

1 reel, 30 min.
sh-ce-gen
NET
Indiana University ($5.40 rental)

"Ku Klux Klan: The Invisible Empire"

Cameras and microphones have gone inside the Klan to
study the aims and mentality of this band of men that
has caused so much havoc in the southern United
States. The torches, hoods, and flaming crosses are part
of their unholy ritual of hate and reign of terror. Included in this chilling document are scenes from, "The
Birth of a Nation," the Civil War epic which purported
to show the Ku Klux Klan as a lawful organization.
Flashing across the screen are the faces of bigots, fana-
tics, lunatics, dulled by ignorance and inflamed by violence.

2 reels, 47 min.
sh-c-adult
CBS News
Carousel Films $250

"The Radical Americans: The Angry Negro"

Examines a number of opinions of Negro leaders as to
the way the Negro should operate in his search for
equality. Includes interviews with Elijah Muhammed
of the Black Muslims; Daniel Watts, editor of *Liberator*
magazine; Jimmy Garrett from the Congress of Racial
Equality; Fannie Lou Hamer, one of the founders of
the Mississippi Freedom Democratic party; John Lewis,
the co-founder, and Julian Bond of the Student Non-
Violent Coordinating Committee; Andrew Young of
the Southern Christian Leadership Conference; and Bill
Epton, candidate from the Progressive Labor party.

1 reel, 30 min.
sh-c-gen
NET
Indiana University ($5.40 rental)

"The Radical Americans: Past, Present, And Future"

Discusses the history of radicalism in the United States
and its possible future effects upon the society. Includes
interviews with Vice President Hubert Humphrey;
Staughton Lynd; Dan Bell, Columbia University; Mich-
ael Harrington of the League for Industrial Democracy;
Norman Thomas; and publisher I. F. Stone. Describes
the probable future of the radical left in this country.

1 reel, 30 min.
sh-c-gen
NET
Indiana University ($5.40 rental)

"The Radical Americans: The Right Takes Over"

Documents the way in which one man can dominate
the thinking of the persons in a town and control their
right to self expression. Introduces Centralia, a one-
factory town, and T. Gano Chance, a member of the
John Birch Society, who runs that factory and controls
the town economically. Presents interviews with persons
from Centralia who describe the economic and social
reprisals directed against them when their ideas do not
agree with Mr. Chance's. Fails to provide an interview
with Mr. Chance because when asked to give his side
of the story he refused.

1 reel, 30 min.
sh-col-gen
NET
Indiana University ($5.40 rental)

"The Radical Americans: Voices From The Right"

Develops the idea that the radical right expresses the fears of many citizens of this country about individual liberty in an increasingly complex and regulated society. Presents some of the people—both some who are well-known and some who are obscure—who speak for the radical right and explain what they stand for and oppose. Examines the various radical right organizations that are legitimate expression of the tradition of radicalism in the country.

1 reel, 30 min.
sh-col-gen
NET
Indiana University ($5.40 rental)

"The Radical Americans: Who Teaches Them?"

Compares schools in America with a radically left or radically right orientation and reveals something about their techniques. Interviews such teachers as Allen Krebs, Director of the Free University of New York; Ed Richer, who tried to found a similar university in Gainsville, Florida; Carolyn Craven of the Students for a Democratic Society; the president of Harding College; and the dean of Rampart College, Larkspur, Colorado.

1 reel, 30 min.
sh-c-gen
NET
Indiana University ($5.40 rental)

"The Radical Right in Southern California"

Presents host Cecil Brown describing in detail six leading right-wing extremist leaders: Robert Welch, Kent Courtney, Willis Stone, Carl McIntire, Gerald Smith, and Robert DePugh. Opens with a brief historical examination of extremist movements in the United States as described by Allan Nevins. Focuses on Southern California and various opposing representative leaders, who openly accuse one another of Communist leanings and bomb threats.

1 reel, 29 min.
sh-c-gen
NET
Indiana University ($5.40 rental)

"Star Spangled Extremists"

Alan F. Westin, professor of law at Columbia University, guides his audience toward a better awareness of radical groups. He places their "cause" in perspective and illustrates their "effect" through historical prints, photographs, and news film. With particular emphasis on today's problems, Prof. Westin examines radical group tactics—book censorship, P.T.A. take-over, character assassination—which are undermining communities across the land. He also demonstrates the similarities and differences between the radical right and left.

1 reel, 28 min.
sh-c-adult
Carousel Films $135
Anti-Defamation League of B'nai B'rith
University of Iowa ($5.00 rental)

"Anti-Semitism In America"

Dr. Melvin Tumin, professor of sociology and anthropology at Princeton University, presents a study in depth of the attitudes and motivations behind anti-Semitism. Dr. Tumin places special emphasis on the "gentle people of prejudice." (Adult and secondary school levels.)

B/W, 25 min.

Cleared for TV.
Anti-Defamation League

"Danger On The Right"

A dramatic documentary, produced by WABC-TV New York, on political extremism. Includes an actual John Birch Society meeting filmed in a suburban community; interviews with top-leaders of the Birch Society and rebuttal of their statements by Dr. Arthur Larsen and ADL officials Benjamin Epstein and Arnold Forster. (Adult and secondary school levels.)

B/W, 59 min.
Cleared for TV.
Anti-Defamation League

"Let Freedom Ring"

Originally broadcast over station WCKT in Miami, Florida, the film deals with the nationwide network of anonymously recorded phone messages known as, "Let Freedom Ring." These messages spread a radical right brand of "fear and smear" in the words of Wyoming's Senator Gale McGee, who appears in the film. Others are Mrs. Jennelle Moorehead, president of the National Congress of Parents and Teachers, which has been under continuing attack by "Let Freedom Ring," and William Pinsley of the Anti-Defamation League of B'nai B'rith, which has filed a complaint with the FCC. The film leaves no doubt that the phone network is simply a new radical right tactic for disseminating the old half truths and lies under a veil of anonymity. (Adult and secondary school levels.)

B/W, 23½ min.
Not cleared for TV.
Anti-Defamation League

"The Radical Right"

This documentary traces the historic background of extremist groups of both the left and the right, with particular stress on the strength of the radical right today. The film starkly exposes who's who and what they stand for in the radical right, identifies the leaders, the sources of their financial support and demonstrates how they infiltrate community groups and disrupt meetings. Victims of their attacks also appear in the film including a minister whose home was bombed, a librarian, and a teacher. An historical analysis of extremism is presented by the noted historian, Professor Allen Nevins. (High school and college students, church and parent-school organizations and all civic-minded fraternal and business groups.)

B/W, 30 min.
Cleared for TV.
Anti-Defamation League

"Society of Bigots?: KKK"

The ABC "Scope" program deals with the Klan in the context of President Johnson's charge that it is "a society of bigots." Howard K. Smith and a crew of ABC reporters cover a Klan rally in the Deep South, interview Imperial Wizard Robert Shelton, and discuss the House Un-American Activities Committee investigation with Attorney General Nicholas D. Katzenbach. As a study of the Ku Klux Klan today, the film forcefully supports the President's charge. (Adult and secondary school levels.)

B/W, 26 min.
Not cleared for TV.
Anti-Defamation League

"Storm Over The Supreme Court"

A vivid portrayal of the history and progress of America's highest court. With films, cartoons, stills, and portraits, it traces the stormy conflict which raged over the Supreme Court from the day of its inception, its influence in major historic events, and the various philosophies and ideologies of its justices. Originally presented as one of the outstanding "CBS Reports" special programs.

Winner of the Peabody Award
B/W, 50 min.
Not cleared for TV.
Anti-Defamation League

"Watts: Riot or Revolt?"

This superb "CBS Reports" documentary on the Watts, Los Angeles, riot during the summer of 1965 examines the situation in terms of the nationwide civil rights struggle. From a completely unbiased point of view, the program presents opinions representing both the Negro and white community as it attempts to answer whether Watts was an irrational riot or a planned revolt stemming from social and economic injustice. Newsreel footage of the clash and interviews with community leaders give enlightened testimony to the problems which created the situation. This film is invaluable for human relations groups. (Adults and secondary school levels.)

B/W, 45 min.
Not cleared for TV.
Anti-Defamation League

"The Nature of Anti-Semitism"

A kinescope in the NBC "Open Mind" series. Panel of Arnold Forster, ADL general counsel; Marie Jahoda,

New York University psychology professor; and Harold Taylor, former president of Sarah Lawrence College discuss various aspects of anti-Semitism. Recently given First Award by Ohio State Institute for Education by Radio-Television. (Adult and secondary school levels.)

B/W, 29 min.
Not cleared for TV.

"The Non-Violent"

This is a stirring dramatization in which a young white college student "bears witness" to a civil rights demonstration. This full-hour drama was originally seen on the popular CBS-TV show, "The Defenders." The principles of free speech and assembly and the constitutionality of public demonstrations are put to the test as the young man insists on standing trial in order to focus attention on the grave injustices and denial of freedom meted out to American Negroes.

An excellent film for college students, church and civic organizations; bar associations may also be interested in the legal aspects of this timely issue.

B/W. 50 min.
Not cleared for TV.